THE BOX FROM BRAUNAU

THE BOX FROM BRAUNAU

IN SEARCH OF MY FATHER'S WAR

JAN ELVIN

AMACOM

AMERICAN MANAGEMENT ASSOCIATION

New York • Atlanta • Brussels • Chicago • Mexico City • San Francisco
Shanghai • Tokyo • Toronto • Washington, D. C.

This publication is designed to provide accurate and authoritative information in regard to the subject matter covered. It is sold with the understanding that the publisher is not engaged in rendering legal, accounting, or other professional service. If legal advice or other expert assistance is required, the services of a competent professional person should be sought.

Library of Congress Cataloging-in-Publication Data

Elvin, Jan.
    The box from Braunau : in search of my father's war / Jan Elvin.
        p. cm.
    Includes bibliographical references.
    ISBN-10: 0-8144-1049-9
    ISBN-13: 978-0-8144-1049-3
    1. Elvin, William John. 2. World War, 1939-1945—Campaigns—France—Normandy. 3. Braunau (Concentration camp). 4. World War, 1939-1945—Concentration camps—Liberation—Austria. 5. United States. Army. Infantry Division, 80th—Biography. 6. Soldiers—United States—Biography. I. Title.

    D756.5.N6E35 2009
    940.54'1273092—dc22
    [B]
                                                        2008039490

Printing Number

10 9 8 7 6 5 4 3 2

To all the veterans of World War II and their families,
and to the memory of my father

CONTENTS

APPENDIX E

PREFACE

Not many combat veterans share their war experiences with their families—at least not the brutal experiences. When was the last time your father insisted you pull up a chair and listen to his war stories? Or complained that no one wanted to hear about the time his best buddy died in his arms? Or talked about the day he killed his first enemy soldier, who turned out to have been about sixteen years old? If he did share these sorts of experiences, you probably got the sanitized version, not the one with all the terrible details.

My father, who fought in World War II, didn't want to talk about his experiences overseas either. Until late in his life, he was unwilling to dredge up long buried memories or inflict their depressing details on us. For years, they lay buried and unspoken.

The war not only changed my father's life but our family's life as well. Although he'd proved his courage and leadership as a junior officer in the infantry, hidden emotional wounds left Dad with symptoms of post-traumatic stress disorder (PTSD). The resulting conflicts in his marriage and the effect his inner turmoil had on his children cast a shadow over the life of a good, wise, and intelligent man.

Dad was eighty-five years old when I accidentally rediscovered an object from the past, a box that had been given to him by a POW in a prison camp in Braunau, Austria, in 1945. The discovery led me to question how he'd come to receive it, and those questions helped me to forge a closer emotional connection with him. His answers provided me with a point of entry into his history. Regrettably, this occurred only a few years before his death. Writing *The Box from Braunau* challenged me to solve the mystery of my father and the box that held such vivid and unforgettable memories for him. The shocking things he revealed were not easy for him to talk about.

Dad didn't enjoy a discussion of feelings. Writer Sue Miller, in *The Story of My Father: A Memoir*, described her father in a way that might have described mine, saying, "He could be more effectively nonresponsive than anyone I've ever known." Like so many World War II veterans, my father was economical in his comments. For example, he would say, "I was company commander for about twenty minutes because the company commander got hit. Then I got hit twenty minutes later, so that was brief." And he never bragged about his Silver Star, preferring to mention his Combat Infantryman's Badge, which signified that he'd served in the Infantry on the front lines. For many soldiers, the Combat Infantryman's Badge was the most respected and treasured decoration.

As Dad's story emerged, it invited me to look more closely into his life. Although this process had its share of troubled moments, it was a pleasure to bear witness to someone I admired and loved so much.

This book is my search for my father's war. I was fortunate to be able to draw upon sources such as Dad's letters from the front, the maps he penciled prior to leading a dangerous patrol, and his war journal, covering combat in France from early August to November 1944, as well as my grandfather's diary and personal interviews I conducted with relatives, other World War II veterans, and concentration camp survivors. My father's letters and firsthand accounts of battle offered me an intimate look at him that I'd never had before.

My initial goal was to describe Dad's war experiences, but I was slow to grasp why writing a book about my father, his war, and our family felt so right. I knew my motive was to get to know him better and deepen my understanding of my childhood and of myself. But I had an "Aha!" moment when it occurred to me that since Dad was a newspaper reporter by trade, writing was his game, and to get to know him, I would need to play it. To track down the "real" Bill Elvin, I interviewed, investigated, wrote, reported, and followed up. Working on his turf gave me license to indulge my curiosity about him, to interview close relatives, and to ask probing questions I otherwise would not have ventured to ask. Somehow, even after his death, I needed his permission to write about him, and this was the way to do it. Researching the story behind the box gave me a way to get to know this enigmatic but beloved figure in my life. Old, half-forgotten memories tumbled over me, some as pleasurable as the smell of lilacs in Virginia, some as disturbing as the chill in the air during family quarrels.

The chapters in this book alternate between Dad's war experiences and his family life, combining history and memoir. In both, I did my best to find the truth. I sought to correlate times, places, and incidents in his war journal with historical records and testimonies of other veterans. I have no doubt gotten some things wrong despite my best efforts. Also, my siblings would each have a different story to tell about our family life, and I'm sure my father would, too. We are bound to see our parents through our own unique lens.

Tim O'Brien, author of *The Things They Carried* and *If I Die in a Combat Zone: Box Me Up and Ship Me Home*, said in an NPR interview in 2004 that a private in the Army has limited vision because, unlike an officer, he has neither maps nor binoculars. He pops his head up out of his foxhole during a firefight, ready to shoot, while an officer must be out in front and aware of what's going on around him. The officer's eyes must remain open. (O'Brien said that as a private in Vietnam, he kept his eyes closed much of the time.) When I first started writing, I was like the private who has little ability to see beyond his foxhole. Blocked by my own history, insecurities, and emotions, my view of much of the action in Dad's life was restricted, working as I was without a map or guide. In a conversation with a friend not long after Dad died, I asked her if she thought I was capable of writing this book. She looked at me and said, "Just get out of the way, Jan. Let your dad do it." And as the story unfolded, gradually, "maps of the terrain" and "vision aids" began to appear and things zoomed into focus: Dad helped me open my eyes.

D-Day fell on June 6, 1944, and sixty days later, on August 5, my father disembarked at Omaha Beach in Normandy, France. The artillery was silent, since most of the Allied fighting force had moved inland to chase the German Army. Still, I imagine Dad felt the tension in the air as he stepped onto the shore and marched up the beach. He was about to become a member of the relatively tiny band of men who saw combat on the ground during World War II. This book winds through his childhood, his journey in World War II, and our life as a family. By writing it, I got back the father I'd lost years ago.

ACKNOWLEDGMENTS

First I want to thank my husband, Al Bronstein, for too many things to mention, but at least for his unfailing faith in me and for cooking dinner; also for good advice, for suffering along with my angst, for taking care of me while I was buried in writing, and for his steadfast love.

Thanks to my terrific editor at Amacom, Bob Nirkind, who was always wise and kind in shepherding me through the process of writing *The Box from Braunau*. I simply could not have asked for a better editor.

Also thanks to Bob DiForio, my agent, who had faith in the project from the start and made things happen.

Ursula Junk, whose devotion to uncovering the truth in history encouraged me to begin writing. I wish she had lived to see it completed.

Special thanks to two highly decorated World War II veterans I'm honored to call friends: Bob Murrell and Walter Carr. Bob Murrell has an encyclopedic knowledge of the doings of the 80th Division, and his patience in answering even the dumbest questions with grace can never be repaid. Walter Carr provided me with the gift of his time and intelligence, but I'm especially grateful to him for sharing memories of my father in wartime, which brought to life a picture of Dad as a young Army officer.

Also to all other veterans of World War II and their family members who offered assistance and friendship, especially George Anderson, Gene Blanchard, Jeannie Davis, Lloyd Jonnes, Bill Kelly, Paul Mercer, Bob Persinger, Leroy Pierce, Joe Scott, Pat Stewart, Clayton Warman, and my adopted F Company family. Getting to know all these veterans has been one of the unexpected pleasures of writing this book.

To Katey Coffing, whose patience and coaching skill guided my writing and invigorated the project. Always ready with help and encouragement, she has been a joy to work with.

Max Garcia, survivor of Auschwitz and Ebensee, for his generosity in allowing me to look into the world he inhabited during the war years and make it public.

Elvin Clan members—including my siblings, aunts, uncles, nephews, nieces, and cousins—for their memories of Dad and their support.

All those who made valuable contributions of encouragement, insight, and information, including Robert Abzug, Meg Calkins, Katie Cogan, Allen Horne, Camilla Lake, Hallie Lovett, Patricia Magee, Tillie McCarren, Bill Prindle, Charles Shields, Anne Wotring, and many others, especially Kathy Fitch and Ruth Prindle.

Andy Adkins for helping me navigate the foreign world of the Army and military matters, but mostly for his inspiration.

My companions in Babes on Bikes, for their interest and conversations while riding the beautiful bike trails of DC.

My neighbor Theo Specht, for German translation.

Bill Hollinger for offering his time and expertise to rejuvenate the photos and maps I used for the book.

Ruth McGoff for sharing her memories of my father and for making him happy. She brought such joy to him and our family.

My son Ben, whose optimism and love for his family always warm my heart.

• • •

Grateful acknowledgment is made of permission to quote materials, including the Holocaust Memorial Center for use of the Herman Roth interview cited in Chapter 9, and Casemate Publishing for use of material from *You Can't Get Much Closer Than This.*

A Box Full of Memories

Nearly thirty years had passed since I'd seen the box my father brought home from World War II in 1946. While visiting my younger brother, George, in the summer of 2003, I saw it again, on George's desk, just the way it had sat on Dad's. I stood next to my brother and ran my fingers over the box's rough surface.

As I touched it, childhood memories flooded over me—how the box had rested atop the big, yellow oak desk in my father's den in our 1950s Arlington, Virginia home. In my mind's eye, I saw him leaning against the desk, with one long leg propped up on the chair. He worked there often, making calls and writing notes for stories. He never referred to himself as a "journalist," preferring the more modest title of "newspaperman." I remembered how he balanced the phone between ear and shoulder while dictating a story to his editor at the Washington *Evening Star* newspaper.

As a child, the box had meant nothing to me—it was just part of the landscape of my father's daily life. And he didn't take to children going into things on his desk. Suddenly, at my brother's house, I wanted to know. What did Dad keep in the box? His poor health made me want to fill in the gaps of what I knew about his life before it was too late. Why had he always guarded his thoughts and feelings so carefully? Did the box hold a key to understanding our father?

"Where did Dad get the box?" I asked, looking up at George. He was so like Dad—tall, quiet, and handsome.

"In the war." In a voice as deep and rich as Dad's, George told me a tale I'd never heard: Toward the end of the war, Dad met a prisoner interned at a German-run camp. The American soldiers freed the inmates, and out of gratitude, this man gave Dad an aluminum box he'd made in the camp. George knew only the skeleton of the story—not the name of the camp or anything about the prisoner.

A picture of my father as a young soldier took shape in my mind. William John Elvin, Jr., known as Bill, was a decorated combat veteran of General George S. Patton's Third Army, 80th Infantry Division. He reached the Normandy beaches sixty days after D-Day as an idealistic twenty-six-year-old first lieutenant who'd left a wife and baby behind to serve his country. He fought and led his platoon bravely, earning not only a Silver Star for Gallantry in Action, but the Combat Infantryman's Badge and a Purple Heart. Before the war had ended, Dad suffered experiences he would have liked to forget, and he stayed silent about them almost until his death. As children, we thought all fathers had nightmares and jumped at loud noises. Like a cat ready to spring, he was always poised for danger. Only as adults did we recognize the traumatic impact war had had on our father.

I picked up the box. Light in weight, it was the length and width of a letter-sized piece of paper and three inches deep. The crude engraving on it looked as though its maker had used a rudimentary tool to hammer out the design. Perhaps using whatever he could find—a rock, or maybe a nail—he made a rustic sketch of a man and a woman on top of the box, surrounded by flowers and ivy. On one side was written "Braunau 1944."

After that visit with George, I returned home to Washington, DC, and my husband, Al Bronstein. Our German friend,

Ursula Junk (pronounced "Yoonk"), was visiting us. As a college student in the 1960s, she'd worked with my husband in the civil rights movement in Mississippi. After she returned to her home in Germany in the early 1970s, Ursula began a career as a radio journalist, creating mostly documentaries. Because of her familiarity with the United States, she traveled here often to do stories while visiting friends. Ursula was an intense, striking blonde who looked much younger than her sixty-plus years and who tempered her intensity with humor. She always talked to my cats in German, interrogating them as though interviewing for a serious story.

At the time of this visit, Ursula was working on a documentary about the American soldiers who liberated Buchenwald, the notorious Nazi concentration camp in Germany. While my husband prepared dinner, she and I sat in the living room and she told me about her fascinating—and horrifying—research on what the soldiers had encountered at Buchenwald in May 1945. Over a glass of wine, I told her what I'd learned from George about the gift the camp inmate had given Dad, and how Dad had kept it for years without ever revealing its meaning or its origin to anyone. She pressed me to find out which camp the box had come from. Had my father's Army unit liberated a concentration camp? The question made the hair stand up on the back of my neck.

After dinner and more talking, I was anxious to find the answer and I phoned Dad at his home in nearby McLean, Virginia. At eighty-five years old, he still enjoyed writing for the weekly newspaper he'd owned and published for thirty years. He'd sold the paper some years ago, but he was still "McLean's newspaperman."

My heart sped up a little when Dad answered the phone. With Ursula's account of the liberation of Buchenwald fresh in my mind, I just assumed that the "camp" George had referred to was a concentration camp. So I asked, "What was the name of the concentration camp you saw during World War II?"

I heard the intake of breath while he pondered the question. Ebensee, he said, a camp in central Austria. His voice trembled as he added, "It was a death camp." He described a scene like those we have all seen—and recoiled from—in photographs of Nazi concentration camps. "I remember running into the woods afterwards and I couldn't see."

"Couldn't see?"

He mumbled something about tears in his eyes. The conversation was getting emotional, and Dad had never been comfortable showing feelings. He wanted to end it quickly, and we hung up after saying only a few more words.

After the phone call I sat in silence for a moment, stunned that I'd never known my father had seen a concentration camp firsthand. Ursula and I then looked at a map of Austria. We found Ebensee where Dad had said, deep in the Salzkammergut region, site of the filming of *The Sound of Music*. The disconnect between the breathtaking scenery and the unspeakable atrocities and sufferings at the camp must have been hard for the American soldiers to absorb, as it was for me. As for Ursula, she was now a reporter on the hunt for a story. She knew that Dad was also a journalist and that his observations would likely be sharper than most witnesses, even fifty-eight years later. She strongly urged me to record an interview with him.

When I was growing up, Dad would tell me the occasional war story. He'd spread out maps on the card table in the living room to demonstrate troop movements. Rolling up his sleeve, he'd show me the scar—a moon-shaped crater on his left forearm—from the wound he received in France on the morning of November 8, 1944. A German sniper aimed his gun and took his shot. Dad felt the heat and the sting, and looking down, saw blood spreading over the front of his jacket. He believed he'd been mortally wounded but discovered to his relief that the wound was on his arm and not in his gut. While recuperating in a hospital in England, he'd close his fist and move it up and down, watching tendons and muscles move, he said, "like railroad tracks," made visible because the German bullet had removed the skin.

Years later, at age 79, Dad found himself confronted with a much more serious medical problem: pulmonary fibrosis, a debilitating and progressive lung disease. I often drove him to the hospital for tests on his decreasing lung capacity. The idea was to see how much he could do, and the respiratory therapists pushed him to the brink of his physical limits. For each appointment, I maneuvered his wheelchair down the long corridor to the pulmonologist's office. After one particularly grueling series of tests, a nurse wheeled him into the waiting room in a state of near collapse and I asked him foolishly, "How was it?" Dad gave me a small smile and whispered, "Well, at least they're not shootin' at me."

Dad and I set up a time for me to interview him. After Ursula left Washington to pursue her Buchenwald story, I mailed him a list of questions so he could prepare for the interview. Ursula kept in touch, urging me to research my father's story. We agreed that his recollections were important because when his generation faded, the story would remain. My purpose for the interview was twofold: I wanted to know more about my father's experiences during the war, but I also wanted to help preserve his memories for future generations. Before the interview could take place, though, he sent me a short, handwritten account of the one day he'd spent at Ebensee. He was more comfortable writing than sitting with me for an interview face-to-face. "After seeing Ebensee," he wrote, "soldiers who had become accustomed to the suffering and ghastly wounds of battle were overcome."

I felt shortchanged. I wanted the freedom to ask my father about what had happened, but now he was controlling the conversation. I picked up the phone and called him. But soon I realized that his voice broke whenever we spoke about Ebensee. He was trying to hold back tears. I had never before heard my father cry.

For years I'd bemoaned Dad's inaccessible emotions, but now I found myself longing for my old "stiff-upper-lip" Dad. That was the man I was accustomed to, and it was jarring to deal with even this hint of his pain. I'm not sure which of us was more uncomfortable. I couldn't bear to hear that break in his voice.

Since I wasn't getting much information from Dad, I took advantage of the access I had to great research institutions. As I studied and learned more, I began to see the camp as he would have on that day of its liberation in May 1945. The Nazi SS, who were the guardians of Ebensee and the torturers of its inhabitants, had fled from the advancing U.S. Army, leaving behind starving, filthy, and ghostlike prisoners, still surrounded by barbed wire.

Meanwhile, I kept going back to the box, puzzling over it and trying to flesh out its mystery. Who was the inmate who gave it to Dad? Why? How was it made? There were so many unanswered questions. The inmates at Ebensee were desperately ill and were worked mercilessly. I could not fathom how anyone there could have kept any belongings. They slept three to a wooden bunk in stark barracks. Eking out the barest existence, they lived from moment to moment. Many succumbed to death, having reached a point long past hope or caring.

Learning that Dad had seen a concentration camp made me shudder. I could hardly bear to look at the photos of the prisoners in the camps, and yet my father had been there—if only for one day—and had fled into the woods in tears. This was not part of the combat lore he'd shared with us.

I remembered that my father had often talked about how wasteful and destructive war was. And yet his military service was part of who he was. He sang rousing Army songs and kept his war souvenirs. As a child, I played with a Nazi flag, a German soldier's helmet, Dad's scuffed combat boots, and an unarmed bazooka shell. My brother John (nicknamed "Jay") and I wanted to play with the German gun—the Luger—most of all, but it was off limits even though Dad had removed the pin. His Army uniform hung in his closet until his death. And like a true infantry soldier, when frustrated, Dad would groan, "Oh, my achin' GI back." (I can just hear him saying it when I told him I'd heard that Richard Nixon had selected Spiro Agnew to be his vice presidential running mate.)

When the question finally crystallized in my mind, I asked Dad, "How could a prisoner at Ebensee have made, or even kept possession of, anything at all?" He surprised me by saying that the box was not from a prisoner at the concentration camp in Ebensee, but from a prisoner in Braunau, Austria, the site of a German-run forced labor camp west of Ebensee. The town of Braunau was notorious as the birthplace of Adolf Hitler. Soldiers of the 80th Division, including Dad, liberated the camp near the end of the war before moving on toward Ebensee.

That explained the inscription, "Braunau 1944," on the side of the box. I had seen those words at George's but they hadn't registered because I'd been so focused on Ebensee. In a way, I was disappointed that the box had not come from Ebensee. I liked a tidy story as much as anyone. But I would find that everything was more complicated than I'd thought— the camps, the war, and its consequences for my father and my family. I felt on the verge of discovery about a man I thought I knew. Now I was no longer sure how well I knew him, but I yearned to learn more.

I could tell by Dad's reference to running into the woods in tears, by the tremor in his voice, and by his reluctance to talk about Ebensee that these were powerful memories. When he shut down the painful thoughts and images of his life as a soldier, had he also shut down other, more positive emotions? Sometimes I felt the war had stolen his exuberance and his innocence from him, and from us. Part of him had remained on those bloody fields and in those haunted mountains.

I clearly imagined my father, tall in his crisp uniform, full of idealism and ready to do his duty for his country. The horrors of war lay ahead, and I knew the future he could not see. I saw him not so much as a father but as the way I would see a son. After all, he was only slightly older then than my own son is now. Through this lens, our lives were inverted—I'm wise and knowing, and he's young and vulnerable. This straight-backed young man was trying so hard to do what was right and was so afraid of disappointing the people in his life. It enlightened me in the same way that giving birth and raising a child gave me an understanding of my mother that I couldn't have gotten otherwise. I forgave my mother for many things in the early years of my own motherhood; now, after learning more about my father, my empathy for him deepened. I began to understand the roots of his emotional penny-pinching, and I began to forgive.

•　•　•

While researching this book, time and again I heard the same refrain from people my age: "My father never talked about it either. He never wanted to." Soon it will be too late to ask the World War II veterans to call up their memories. Estimates of the number of World War II soldiers who die each day range from 1,000 to 1,500. Time is short. If we want to know about their experiences, we need to ask while we still can.

Asked to evaluate the effect of the war, Dad said:

I wouldn't be surprised if a hundred years from now historians and other analysts will say that World War II, like World War I, was just a terrible cruel waste, a terrible infliction of suffering on millions and millions of people that never needed to happen . . . if people had been wiser, more unselfish, more tolerant, and had a broader view of what was needed.

It isn't just the veterans who are hesitant to speak of war in personal terms. Some vets have told me, "My children have never *asked* me about the war. I'd tell them if they asked." One eighty-one-year-old Army veteran, pretending to make a joke of it, said, "I'm an object of ridicule in my family when I talk about the war." Could the reluctance to open up the war experiences for real discussion be mutual? To venture down the path of a father's past is not easily done, but in my case, it was healing; it can be for others as well. I wish I had become curious sooner. Dad might have disclosed more had there been time.

But I did succeed in finding out quite a bit. Just before he died, he showed me the remarkable journal he kept that describes his first three months of combat in 1944. I've read it many times, and it's helped me understand why the war left him so unsettled for the remainder of his life. The excerpts I've included in this book make compelling reading for the story they tell of life at the battlefront. And eight months after he passed away, I attended the sixtieth anniversary commemoration of the liberation of the concentration camp at Ebensee by the Americans. There, I became friends with some of the liberating soldiers and survivors of the camp. Exactly one year after Dad's death, I attended a reunion of the 80th Infantry Division and met some of the men who had fought with him. Through my research, I learned that combat veterans have a string of traits in common—anxiety, depression, sleeplessness, sensitivity to loud noises, inability to maintain close relationships, night-mares, and hypervigilance—some of which last only a short while, some a lifetime. In addition, many casualties of war fail to appear in the statistics—casualties that should be listed—such as the soldiers' children. The children of America's "Greatest Generation" have shared an inheritance of silence and hidden wounds for sixty years.

Of course, it doesn't end with the offspring of World War II veterans. The children of Vietnam vets are now adults. Soldiers have come back from the Gulf War and return daily from Afghanistan and Iraq. These families, like mine, struggle to deal with the aftermath of the battlefield and the scars it has inflicted.

Like most veterans of battle, my father talked about his bodily injuries but never his emotional ones—the terror of combat, the deeply felt loss of friends, the shock of the atrocities he witnessed. These invisible wounds went far deeper than the physical ones.

I asked Dad why the prisoner in Braunau had given him the box. He paused, looking off into the distance as if trying to re-capture the moment, and said, "He wanted to show us how grateful he was to be free." That one gesture, representing a captive's yearning for freedom, symbolized what my father and his fellow soldiers were fighting for. It validated their sacrifices and perhaps mitigated his conflicting emotions about the war. Yet the same box that he treasured also held the painful memories that we, his family, knew haunted him by day and certainly by night. When he was finally able to share the memories and secrets of the box, his old wounds—and our family's—could be cared for and healed.

THE BOX FROM BRAUNAU

"Which of us has looked into his father's heart?"
—Thomas Wolfe, *Look Homeward, Angel*

CHAPTER ONE

"Mark Your Socks"

"All well and safe. Writing. All my love."
—Telegram from Dad to my mother, July 28, 1944

From my father's war journal:

JULY 24, 1944—Our welcome to the European Theater of Operations was voiced by one Major Baresi, Coast Artillery, on a forlorn hillside in Wales.

"Greetings, gentlemen, this pleasant Sunday morning. Welcome to the European Theater of Operations, and don't forget to mark all your clothing because lots of times all they find is a leg. If your leggings and socks have your name and serial number on them, you will be more or less promptly identified.

"At the rate they're chewing up officers over on the Far Shore—that's France, if you don't know—you may leave here by plane early tomorrow morning. You may be in combat by noon, and if you are one of the lucky, be back in a hospital in England by nightfall.

"The Germans are knocking out officers far faster than we can replace them. It's time for you men to settle down with a field manual and learn all you can in the few hours that are left to you."

Major Baresi's address became a standing joke as we moved through England to Southampton, across the Channel, and up Omaha Beach on D-Day plus 60.

This was the opening passage of the journal my father wrote in 1945 while stationed in Germany and Czechoslovakia with the Army of Occupation. Although the journal begins in 1944, soldiers were not allowed to keep a journal in combat for fear it might fall into enemy hands, so Dad must have actually written it the next year. Perhaps he made notes during battle, tucking them into the breast pocket of his uniform, just behind the picture he carried of my mother, and completed his entries the following year. Dad told me he didn't want the journal published until after his death. I believe he was anxious about having mentioned specific names, never wanting to offend anyone—least of all the men who'd fought by his side in wartime.

Listening to Major Baresi that day were the GIs slated to replace soldiers who'd been killed, wounded, or transferred elsewhere. My father was soon assigned to the 80th Infantry Division, also known as the "Blue Ridge" Division. Its insignia of a white-bordered shield of gold emblazoned with three azure mountain peaks symbolized the three states of the Appalachian region—Pennsylvania, Virginia, and West Virginia—from which the majority of the 80th Division personnel were drawn, although many came from neighboring states such as Maryland and Ohio. As a replacement officer, Dad had not yet been assigned to a particular regiment within the Division.

The replacements boarded ships to carry them across the choppy English Channel from Southampton, England, to Normandy, France. Once they arrived with heavy gear on their backs, they climbed thirty feet down the cargo netting on the side of the boat and jumped into the landing craft for transport to French soil. Advancing through the Lorraine region toward the Moselle River, in eastern France, they moved along roads that were easy to traverse thanks to the mild and dry summer weather. The rain would descend soon enough, turning the roads to thick, viscous mud. Optimism rose among the Allied troops as reports of a dispirited and disorganized German Army filtered back from the front. The rumors flew everywhere: The Germans were withdrawing to the Siegfried Line (the system of heavy fortification on the border of Germany); the Germans were withdrawing to the Rhine.

General Omar Bradley issued instructions not to send winter clothing to the front so that space on trucks coming overland from French ports could be used for gasoline and supplies. He believed the war would be over by winter and the clothes wouldn't be needed. On August 23, the SHAEF (Supreme Headquarters Allied Expeditionary Force) announced, "The August battles have done it and the enemy in the West has had it. Two-and-a-half months of bitter fighting have brought the end of the war in Europe in sight, almost within reach." The Allies were clearly unaware that the German Army was determined to make a stand at the Moselle River and to turn Allied optimism to defeat.

AUGUST 1944—The trip across France was trucks flying over dusty roads and camps in the pleasant countryside. And always rumor, rumor, rumor. From the time of our first camp near the beachhead, there were reports of what units we were going to join and when. But Patton kept on moving, and it was September before the grim nervousness in men's faces told us we were near the fighting front.

The Last Ride was a gloomy affair highlighted by the driver getting lost and wondering right out loud if he was still on our side of the line. While all this was going on, somebody picked up a droning overhead and there was a mad scramble while the blackout lights were turned off. We waited an eternity while the planes passed over. Someone said, "Them's Heinies," [GIs frequently referred to the Germans as Heinies, Krauts, or Jerries.] *but Ellsworth, who had been in combat with the British Eighth Army, said in his don't-give-me-that-stuff manner that you can't identify a plane by its motor alone.*

Eventually we pulled off into a field where we pitched tents. Even Ellsworth and Graham pitched, too, because they'd had a most miserable night about a week before when Ellsworth had scouted the sky and decided it would be a good night to sleep under the stars. They had gotten wet, along with all their equipment, much to the delight of those of us who had labored to erect a shelter.

We were now at 80th Division Rear, which has a sweet sound to any front-line 80th man. Anything between Division Rear and Battalion Forward is generally much to be desired. After the usual waiting around, we were moved along to Regimental Rear, where we were met by the Graves Registration Officer [charged with identification and proper burial of the dead in battle]. *He said he had been having a busy day. We were impatient to get settled but at the same time, the real thing was getting too close for comfort. Ellsworth had been assigned to the 317th, so Graham and I were boosting each other's morale in the 318th.*

My father and First Lieutenant Norval Graham were old friends from Frostburg, Maryland, where Dad had grown up. On the long Jeep rides through the countryside under the hot August sun, he and Dad talked—not only about what lay ahead, but about home.

The first question one soldier asked another was always, "Where're you from?" Talking to a GI about where he was from provided an instantly warm topic, and friendships came easier with a soldier from one's home state. For Dad, "home" meant both Frostburg and Cumberland, two adjacent towns sheltered by the Appalachian Mountains.

Graham was sent to F Company and I was assigned to E Company. The kitchens were adjacent and we had a good meal. Sergeant Conroy [the Mess Sergeant] fed one well and I was glad to be back in an outfit again and rid of the anonymous and ominous title "replacement officer."

My father was now officially a first lieutenant in General George S. Patton's Third Army, 80th Infantry Division, 318th Regiment, 2nd Battalion, E Company. In the early phases of the campaign, the men of the 80th lived up to their motto, "The 80th Only Moves Forward." They encountered pockets of resistance, demolitions, and minefields, but along the way they were also able to rest their eyes on the smooth green landscape of France. Passing by patches of pumpkins and melons, grapes on the vine, and forests of fir trees, they spied cattle but few horses—the Germans had taken most of them to use for transportation. After General Patton's fuel supplies dried up the Americans may have wished they had taken the horses first.

The gasoline shortages had begun to slow them down. When Patton couldn't obtain any more gasoline, he told his troops to go ahead with what they had. "Walk!" he ordered, adding, "My men can eat their belts, but my tanks gotta have gas."

Patton's fuel crisis eased, however, in early September when the Division captured desperately needed gasoline, allowing them to replenish their gas tanks and hasten their drive toward the Moselle River. Their objective was to lay a bridge crossing at the Moselle so the tanks of the 4th Armored Division could reach the east bank of the river and then go on to capture the city of Nancy. But the delay caused by the gasoline shortage had created a serious problem. It had allowed the Germans time to dig in and prepare for the oncoming American fighters. The elite German Panzer Division, waiting at almost full strength, was able to stock up on supplies and establish excellent observation sites from Mousson Hill above the Moselle River Valley.

From these high vantage points, the Germans could pinpoint any movement on or near the river, starkly exposing the Americans to artillery attack.

The replacements finally reached the front lines.

We rode for miles over an amazing network of muddy, country roads. The farther we went, the more noise we heard from the artillery of both sides and the more guns and tanks became visible, partly concealed in gullies and woods. We were bug-eyed and rather enjoying the whole thing until we passed the Battalion Aid Station, where ambulances were whirling in and out continuously. A soldier standing by the road was pleading with everyone coming from the rear for water for the Aid Station.

The Battalion CP [Command Post] was down in a bowl in a thick, young wood. Several enlisted men and a Captain, looking weary unto death, were sitting there, using the radio and phone and marking the map. The Jerries started shelling the other side of the road from where we were, and with the first, low whistle, everyone hit the ground. The first one sounded as if it was coming right in; the ones that followed did, too, but they all had enough oomph to carry them over the ridge.

The situation was not good. A Colonel and the General came in and the Captain reviewed the whole picture. We were treated to a full resume of the action of the previous 24 hours and of the positions of each of the companies. The Battalion situation was still bad from the day before. Each company was isolated from each of the others and all attempts at reorganization and supply had met withering opposition.

About noon we went out of the woods and hopped on a jeep, which took us to the Battalion Observation Post. There I met Cumberland, Maryland's Colonel John Golden. He told us that the company commanders were coming back to get the attack order. Nobody was straying far from a good, substantial slit

*trench. With food and ammunition running low, something had
to be done.*

*The answer was simple and the General gave it: Attack!
Graham and I looked at each other. Graham looked as though
he were on the way to the Chair. I must have looked about the
same; that's how I felt.*

The Americans were faced with a run of foul weather, a formidable German defense, and the triple geographical obstacles of
a canal, a river, and a river valley. Strategic military decisions,
made in haste, coupled with poor reconnaissance and lack of artillery and fighter-bomber support, led to the failure of the initial plan. The flood plain offered no cover, and drenching rains
created a dangerous river with a racing current that overflowed
its banks. Moreover, the enemy had revitalized and regained its
iron-jawed determination. The American infantry was accustomed to racing across France with relative ease, with tanks out
in front to forge their path. Now they were vulnerable, but they
didn't realize how vulnerable. When the 317th Regiment
reached the riverbank in early September 1944 and attempted
to cross in broad daylight, hopelessly exposed, German mortars
and machine-gun fire destroyed many of their boats. Many men
were lost, either drowned or killed by enemy fire. They
valiantly tried again toward nightfall, but it was impossible.

Over the next few days, in a complete revision of the original plan, 80th Division Commander Major General Horace L.
McBride fixed on two crossing sites near Dieulouard, France, a
small town on the west bank of the Moselle. The Division was
better prepared this time. Dad's regiment, the 318th, would follow the 317th in the early morning crossing, its aim to occupy
high ground in the northern portion of the bridgehead. It
would take longer than McBride or anyone else anticipated to
accomplish the feat of establishing the bridgehead.

On September 4, the 318th began its attack on Hill 326 in

a drizzling rain overlooking Marbache, just south of Dieu-louard. Dad's E Company was ready to support the attack.

They incurred heavy casualties. Companies E and G braved enemy small arms fire, many automatic weapons, mortars, and 20mm guns while crossing open terrain and storming up the hill to secure valuable high ground.

The company commander was Captain Bob Matlick, also from Cumberland. He didn't look well and the men said he was still suffering from a wound he got at Argentan. We sat under a bush and waited for the remnants of the company to come down off "The Hill."

We would also have the mission of protecting some tank destroyers. Captain Matlick pointed to the area, perhaps half a mile away, where I was to find the TDs—tank destroyers. When the men arrived, I moved them off the path and told them to rest while the sergeant and I went out to locate the TDs.

That was the first meeting with Sergeant Roberts; we were to see much of each other until the day in Rouves when he was killed, a few minutes before I was wounded. The immediate problem was simple. There were three guns and I set up an arc defense around each one, with greater strength on the exposed right flank and a small reserve near me in case of trouble. Every once in a while a shell would whistle over, so the men took their positions quickly and dug rapidly. They knew we were lucky to be back a bit but shelling was always a danger, and the night before the Jerries had sneaked in and captured two TDs, so no one was relaxing.

Not far from the road on our left was a natural hole about the size of a slit trench, so I reserved that. The TD lieutenant invited me to share his CP down the hill in a stone shelter behind a house, but I declined. I wanted to get along with the men and, I might add, I didn't know any better at the time.

Toward the middle of the night I slept by fits and starts, awakened continually by the cold and, no doubt, excitement and uneasiness.

The heavy enemy counterattacks on the 318th Regiment continued in the area, still on the west side of the Moselle, of Marbarche, and the Forêt de l'Avant Garde, but the Americans dug in and held the high ground. Meanwhile, other troop elements of the 80th began to cross the river. *Stars and Stripes,* the Armed Forces newspaper, described their early efforts on September 8th:

> There was a bloody battle in one spot on the rain-swept Moselle River last night. Soaking wet in drenching rain, they waded down to the river edge, plunged waist deep into the water, and started to cross with a good chance of never making the far bank . . . Here was the invasion all over again . . . We have got so used to tanks rushing ahead boldly, knocking a pathway for the infantry to move up with what at the time seemed agonizing slowness to correspondents riding through territory uncleared except for the armored drives—but there are times when the tanks must wait for the infantry to open a hole . . . One such time is when the enemy is entrenched across a river, with anti-tank guns commanding the water barrier. Such was the scene here.[1]

SEPTEMBER 10, 1944—As the morning passed and our clothes began to dry out, we could see tanks and troops moving up and across our front to attack. There was much shelling and firing to our right front, but finally, late in the morning, word came back that the town was taken. F and G Companies had pushed to the banks of the Moselle River without a casualty.

Prisoners and civilians started coming up the roads, moving to our rear. Jeeps began flying by. Junior, the Cub artillery observation airplane, moved ahead of us a considerable distance, no longer dodging air bursts from the enemy. All sounds of shelling and firing ceased.

About noon, word came back that we were relieved. Dozens of planes were coming over, running up the Moselle and dropping their bombs on the other bank. After them came dozens more. Everything was a holiday atmosphere. The news that we were to go back was a real tonic to veterans of The Hill, and only a few who had lost close buddies remained cheerless.

Back in the rest area, only a few miles, the Red Cross Clubmobile was waiting and everybody lined up for coffee. By order of the Battalion commander, E Company was to line up first. That may seem a small thing, but it gave the men a boost.

The next morning there were other officers to join the company Carr, Blanchard, and White. Lt. Chmar was exec, or second in command. Later, Lt. Santner arrived and we had two officers for one platoon. I was assigned to the fourth, or weapons, platoon, which was considered a good deal, as good deals go in a rifle company.

Moods darkened as the rain fell ceaselessly, the weather cooled, and battle loomed closer. When alone with his thoughts, Dad reflected on the men who had been killed in combat, and he weighed his own chances for survival. Home was very much on my father's mind the evening before the Division began the perilous crossing of the Moselle.

SEPTEMBER 11—I thought of the GI I had seen the day before, lying as if asleep on the hillside. His uniform was clean and he was wearing a neat-looking pack; he had been moving toward the enemy when some big stuff caught him. The sergeant had wanted to take out the soldier's pocketbook to see if he knew him but I talked him out of it. A picture of a wife or a son might have been too much.

A wife and a son—Dad thought constantly of his wife, Jane, and son, Jay, who was only a toddler. He wrote a letter to Jay to be read only if he died in battle. Wondering if he'd see his family again, he wrote:

> Dear Son,
> Many times I have thought to write this letter but it promised to be difficult and besides I do not choose to burden your mother with words of this vein. I am not pessimistic, but after all, being an officer in a rifle company comes under the heading of hazardous occupations. Please be sure that I have no wish to lay a restrictive hand on what you decide to do or become; I would not have you feel that you were breaking faith with me, no matter what your calling or beliefs. You will have the wonderful advantage of knowing how all this turned out and you will be able to look back with some understanding. I can only tell you what I feel now and what I believe now. Not many of life's problems are simple and war is surely among its most defying complexities, but I don't think it's too naive or idealistic to say that Prime Minister Chamberlain stripped the issue to its essentials when he said at the very beginning, "It is the evil things we will be fighting against." You will learn about me from your mother, from the Elvins, and from my books. You will know that I held in high regard Franklin Roosevelt, Keats, and A. E. Housman. I realize that I have the sharpened appetite and appreciation of the soldier and I know that a person can't go around perpetually counting his blessings, but I do urge you not to take the good things of life for granted. If you find yourself bickering during one of your mother's delicious dinners, if you realize you are unaware of the beauty of a spring day, if you are reading so many books, seeing so many movies, meeting so many people that you are not doing justice to each experience, go off in a corner for a while, take a trip—or just slow down. It is understandable that you should regret that we

will not share the experiences we might have shared together, but do not grieve for me. I was fortunate above most men in having the guidance and encouragement of a mother and father of the sort of which the world needs far, far more. And in your mother's love and my love for her I found a fulfillment and a happiness such as few men could know if they lived a dozen lifetimes. It is hard to believe that any person or group of people could be so bad as to threaten that if they do not have their way, you may never come home at night to a wonderful wife and son, you may never thrill to his enjoyment of your reading *Treasure Island*, never stop at Iron Hill for three double ice cream cones, never arise early at Deep Creek to watch an early summer dawn. You will never know all the dreams and plans that run through my mind through the day and the night; it seems incredible that you and I and your mother might be denied all these things but maybe it helps you to see how the enemy could be so sure that we would never fight.

Dad and his fellow soldiers tried to prepare for the fiercest battle they had yet faced, one that none of them would ever forget. The 318th's turn to fight its way across the Moselle began in rain and darkness.

Later that same night, September 11:

There was some cognac around and we had a few drinks before going to bed. We got into a discussion of what the future held for us as individuals; everyone had a dread but also an unshakable confidence: everything would come out all right.

Not long after I had gone to bed, a runner came up to tell Captain Matlick to report to Battalion CP. At three o'clock all the officers were awakened and given the attack order: Prepare to move to an assembly area for the attack on Dieulouard on the Moselle.

Getting the platoon organized in the dark was a trying job, but we were ready in time. We moved out single file, keeping closed up to avoid losing contact. After some stop and go, we swung down the road, in what Fort Benning called the "approach march." We stopped and started innumerable times but no one was in a hurry now. At one of the stops I ran into Graham and we had a short, excited conversation. We were rather surprised to see each other alive and felt that if we could last for three days we could last for three hundred.

After passing through F Company, Easy [E] Company moved into a long field and deployed facing Dieulouard and the Moselle. The jeep came up and I checked rations and ammunition; each of us took at least one grenade. Then we sat down and waited.

No one wanted to wait and no one wanted to go. The casualties of the last week had all the men on edge and the sound of shells landing in Dieulouard didn't boost morale at all. Trying to decide when to leave a cover and get going was like a game; Jerry was usually obliging, though. If you got cover from the first shell of a barrage, you could just hold tight for a few minutes till he finished with that part of his schedule.

The men were saying that the 317th had crossed ahead of us. We moved all the way to the canal without any trouble at all. Prisoners were filing by with their hands clasped behind their heads; ambulances were running back and forth. The bridge had, of course, been blown up but the engineers had shoved debris into the canal (we thought at the time it was the river), so we crossed without incident. Then there was a wide stream, which we waded carefully, after placing our cigarettes in our helmets. Everything was as quiet as a Sunday afternoon in Vermont.

This, said an engineer who was very proud of himself, was the Moselle. We followed it for perhaps a half-mile to where there was a dam with a very narrow footpath across it.

Everyone was thinking the same thing: Will Jerry start shelling just as I hit the middle? There were shell holes around showing where Jerry had zeroed in.

I dashed across as swiftly as I could, compatible with not falling off, and breathed the usual sigh of relief when I reached the relative shelter of a small bluff on the other side. After we had moved off several hundred yards down the road, we could hear shells landing at the crossing. We looked at each other.

The ground and trees along the river were scarred as if by fire and lightning; no doubt some of the damage, even most, was accomplished by our air corps and artillery. But the sight was not heartening; the limb of a tree, the limb of a man. There was much confusion about where we were to go into position. The day was clear and everything seemed quiet, but a number of the officers seemed very much concerned about a counterattack. Ahead of us was a steeply rising hill, hardly a mountain but a huge ridge-like hill that stretched far to the left and right.

I was digging my combat foxhole and my hands began to get raw very soon. I wanted a smoke and I wanted to rest, but every once in a while black, ominous smoke from a German shell would sprout in the valley behind us, and all the shovels would start flying with superhuman vigor. The company commander's last words were urgent and serious: get the platoon dug in, get the weapons sited, we were sure to be counterattacked.

As soon as my father finished digging his foxhole, the company commander sent him on a mission to find another platoon at a roadblock near Loisy and to bring them back. He doubled back to the river, taking note of the wire entanglements and booby traps the Germans had set up. When he got there, he found that Loisy was deserted. Dad was beginning to worry he'd gotten the wrong directions about the location of the platoon when a voice shouted from the bushes, "Get down, they've been shooting at us." He had found the platoon.

I told them they were to come back with me. They were glad, even though they didn't know, any more than I did, where we would end up. They were all very slow and hesitant on the way back; I was in a hurry because it seemed to me we would be much safer with the rest of the company. We had to hit the ground often now. Jerry was really laying it in all along the river and he was doing a good job on the level ground between the river and the hill. When we came to the wire and booby traps, nobody wanted to move, so Blanchard and I went ahead. The possibility of buried traps hadn't bothered me on the way down the river but it just takes one heeby-jeeby artist to get everybody upset.

It was getting dark when Dad got the platoon back to the company area. But there was no company. E Company had moved out. Colonel Golden asked him how many men he had and then told him to set up a right flank to guard his Command Post. That night ended quietly, but the next several days would see the worst artillery barrage yet, some of the most bitter fighting in the entire European Theater of Operations. Territory exchanged hands several times. The infantry fought fiercely, hill by hill, tree by tree, clawing their way back to regain land only to lose it again, and then begin the exhausting struggle all over again.

The Germans soon recovered from their momentary surprise and launched an all-out, brutal counterstrike at the Moselle.

Finally I did fall asleep. I woke up once to find a vehicle stopped within two or three feet of me. The driver said he didn't know there was anyone dug in around there. I stayed awake till all sounds of vehicles ceased, then went back to sleep.

My awakening was sudden and dramatic. Artillery, flares, burp guns; noise and lights, beautiful to watch and listen to, terrorizing only because of the desperate warnings of the brain.

I lay in my foxhole, shaking from fear and cold. The large caliber fire was zooming right through our position, but that could come from a long way off. None of the guns around me was firing; I couldn't hear a voice. There was hell to pay up on the hill and both the right and left flanks were in trouble but nothing was happening close to us, except that the tracers whistled down into our area and made it advisable to stay down.

I had just given myself this momentous assurance when it began. It's the most helpless feeling in the world: you can't stay and you can't go. You lie all tense and grit your teeth and wait; just as you hear the screech and clench yourself down as far as you'll go, it lands like compressed thunder and lightning. You hear the hot steel flying over your foxhole and all the breath leaves your body; you've survived another one.

They had our field zeroed in but good. I thought the first four or five were close but the next one came tearing through the air as if it were reaching right for me and exploded with such violence that I vibrated from the shock. The next one came in fast, just over me, just as close. The next one would be it. I heard it coming; it landed what seemed like inches from my foxhole and even though it didn't explode, the force of the shell itself turned me around.

Right behind me there was a gigantic thunderclap—no whirr, no whine, no whistle. It was a gun from our own artillery, not 50 yards away, firing back. Now Jerry would try to put that gun out of action. But it was good to have somebody pelting back at him.

The intensity of the artillery fire had drowned out the small arms, but now they could be heard and not far away.

The Schmeizers would brrrrrrup brrrrrrrrp buuuuuurp; our heavies would reply, defiantly, confidently, hubahubahubahubahubahub, hubahubahubahubahubahub. There were other noises—whishes and wheeeeeengs and baaaaaLOOM and uuuuuuuuaaaaaaaaa. Everything was going full blast, tracers and flares everywhere.

I knew that the situation was serious; I had been awakened at one-thirty and I had realized that we weren't up against a routine dawn attack or a patrol. There was still no sign of the dawn. I heard men running down the hill on my left. Before very long, the quick thud-thud of men moving swiftly off the hill could be heard on all sides. Finally, what seemed like a whole company stampeded past us on the right, all yelling, it seemed.

I was getting worried and alarmed and scared. The horror of an artillery attack, when it's concentrated and you don't have the time to think, is animal and personal. This was different; I was fearful of I didn't know exactly what.

There was a fierce exchange going on to our left and to our right and almost to our right rear. Friend and enemy were slugging it out at close range. The enemy line of attack was moving down the hill. A soldier came from the left and I asked him what was going on in the Battalion CP. He said that there was nobody there, that they had gone and we were the only ones left. I found out later that Colonel Golden—he got the Silver Star for it—had been all along the line that night helping keep our forces organized.

Everybody was yelling. I could see—or sense—that the men were looking all around and looking at me, but they all stayed in position. I heard a yell louder than the rest, and it had a familiar ring: "Lootenant Elwin, Lootenant Elwin, we have orders to withdraw to the road." It was Blanchard, down at the end of the line; I didn't have to relay the message to the men. We were up and away almost as soon as the sound of his voice died away. There was nothing like a line at the road; everybody was moving back to the river. I tried to keep our group together but bullets were flying all around us, tracers were whishing past, flares showed us as if it were daylight.

At the bridge they started to go over; I said, no, we're staying here to see if we could make contact with somebody. Just then I ran smack into Graham and we practically embraced each other. He told me that they had taken over the roadblock beyond Loisy and the Jerries had kicked them the hell out. He kept saying, "Goddam bazookaman, goddam bazookaman. I wish to hell I'd had that bazooka."

Graham told me a Jerry tank had come down the road. The crew had got out and shouted, flashed lights, lighted cigarettes, and otherwise invited trouble. From all along the road I had walked down in the afternoon, Heinies had risen to join them. The bazookaman had refused to fire at the tank; it would have been virtual suicide. Graham was as excited as I was but neither of us could figure out what the hell was going on.

We agreed we should stay on this side of the river as long as we had some troops with us.

I turned around; our men were gone.

The MP at the bridge said the whole goddam battalion was back in Dieulouard. He had a most resigned air: the Heinies had kicked the stuff out of the 318th.

NOTE

1. John Wilhelm, "Yanks Fight Bloody Battle to Cross Moselle in Rain: Infantrymen Open Hole for Patton's Tanks to Go Through," *Stars and Stripes 4*, No. 265 (September 8, 1944).

CHAPTER TWO

The Golden Boy

"The time you won your town the race
We chaired you through the market-place;
Man and boy stood cheering by,
And home we brought you shoulder-high."
—A. E. Housman, "To an Athlete Dying Young"

"It was another year of greatness." Dad recorded those words in the journal he kept in 1935, his last year of high school in Frostburg, Maryland. The Beall High School yearbook lists an impressive variety of activities next to his picture: newspaper editor, president of the student body, member of the soccer and track teams, member of the debate team, declamation contest winner for the school, and lead actor in several plays. Yet as I leafed through the pages of the old yearbook, I thought of the high expectations that had been heaped on my father, and I felt sad. I thought of the ways he'd been wounded later in his life and felt a catch in my throat when I read what the yearbook staff had written next: "Hail the Conquering Hero Comes."

Dad was the oldest of Jim and Annie Elvin's four children: Bill, Catherine (Kay), Georgie, and Mary. Dad's father, William John Elvin—known as "Jim"—was born in 1893 and grew up in the tiny Scottish lowlands village of Durisdeer near Dumfries. Jim's father, William Francis Elvin, worked on the railroad and served with the legendary Black Watch Regiment of Scotland in the First Boer War. William Francis and his wife both died young, leaving my grandfather Jim as the orphaned head of household when he was just in his teens—in charge of two brothers and two sisters. Jim's brother George, a brawny, fair-haired, 6'4" lad, walked out of the house at age nineteen and never returned. He had already run away once to fight in World War I at fifteen, but had been brought back when authorities discovered how young he was. More recently, he'd talked about joining the British Army during the Black and Tan War with Ireland. Jim never stopped hoping George would return, especially after slim hints of his whereabouts emerged from places like Hong Kong, Australia, and South Africa. Later, Jim's wife, Annie, described her young brother-in-law George as easy-going and "the one everyone loved the most."

Jim's public school education had been interrupted early so he could care for the family, but after completing correspondence courses in engineering, he got a job as engineering assistant at the Dumfries Peat Factory. In Scotland, everyone from the farmer to the shipyard worker was interested in politics, and Jim was no exception. He was a member of the Labor Party and was in favor of the workingman's right to unionize. His status as sole support of the family prevented him from being drafted into World War I, and eventually he became a manager of His Majesty's Munitions Works in Gretna, near Dumfries, where he met my grandmother, Annie Watt Davidson. One of nine children, she had left her home in Peterhead at sixteen to work in the munitions plant. Peterhead was a small fishing village on the North Sea, near Aberdeen, where her father was a cooper, making barrels for storing fish. The fact that she was from the north of Scotland and Jim was from the south fomented a good-natured rivalry that was an endless source of jabs back and forth throughout their marriage.

They were married while World War I was still going on, and my father was born on Valentine's Day, 1918. My grandmother always said the bells rang out at Greyfriars Church in Dumfries at the very moment my father was born. The bells hinted at what was to come. "He was our golden boy," she'd say, making no attempt to hide the pride in her voice.

One year later, Kay was born just as the calamitous flu pandemic of 1918–1919 had reached its height. Both my one-year-old father and my grandmother Annie had come down with it just at the time she gave birth to Kay. When Annie's mother voiced concern that Annie was tending to "wee William" more than to her newborn, Annie replied, "I don't *know* her, but I know him, and he's sick."

The Gretna plant closed after the war, and Jim entered into a career with the Celanese Corporation that spanned forty years. The company, formed during World War I to produce fabric for airplane manufacture, ensured its postwar success by changing the focus of its production from cellulose acetate film to a new cellulose acetate for use in fabric—a low-cost fiber, called the "beauty fiber," because it was used in satin, brocade, and taffeta. This was a major contribution to the modern textile industry. Jim was asked to join the engineering team at the plant in England, and the family lived in Derbyshire for the next six years.

While there, from across a field sprinkled with buttercups, Dad often watched as the trains chugged by on the tracks behind the house, and he listened for their long, slow whistles. He and Kay attended school in Derbyshire, where they began each day by singing "God Save the King." Their baby brother, Georgie, was too young for school.

After they had spent six years in Derbyshire, Jim walked in

the door one day and asked Annie, "How would you like to go to America?"

Jim had been chosen to start up the new Celanese plant in Cumberland, Maryland, so Annie, Dad, Kay, and Georgie took the train to Peterhead to bid farewell to Annie's family. As they sat in front of the fireplace in the house where Annie had grown up, they knew it could be a long time before they were all together again. The room was filled with sadness, but the story was a familiar one: Scots had been leaving for generations, and those who would be separated could only hope there would be later meetings sometime, somewhere. There was no work in Scotland after World War I, and they knew how fortunate they were that Jim had a job with a good company. Plus, Jim was ambitious, worked hard, and was eager to move up.

• • •

In the summer of 1924, the *Majestic*, the largest and fastest ocean liner in the world at the time, sailed from Southampton, England, to New York, carrying Annie and the three children. Jim had gone ahead on an earlier ship. The Atlantic crossing took only three-and-a-half days, which was sensational for that time, even taking into account the cloudless, pleasant weather. Annie made sure the children knew that many immigrants to the United States at that time had a far less enjoyable crossing. The ship's manifest says that Dad was a "six-year-old Scotch male" and confirms that they were neither anarchists nor polygamists.

To my father, being on board the massive ship was like standing on a mountaintop overlooking the vast and glassy sea. He spent much of his time running around the ship with a friend he'd made, until one of the crewmen came by and told them that little boys who didn't behave might end up overboard in the huge basket he was carrying.

Standing on the deck, at last they spotted the New York skyline. Thrilled by the sight of the city and the Statue of Liberty, the children felt great excitement at the prospect of their new lives in America. The young family settled into the sheltered highlands of Western Maryland, in the town of Frostburg. Frostburg is located at the head of the Georges Creek Valley in the Allegheny Mountains, at the eastern edge of Big Savage Mountain. Soon a new baby, Mary, was born.

In setting up the new plant, Jim often worked twenty-four-hour days. He had the reputation for always being on hand if there was a problem. But the family found time to play together, too. Annie had a lively and sharp wit that was often punctuated by an infectious giggle. Dad's fun-loving sister Kay was always looking for something to get mixed up in. Georgie was mischievous, sweet and—like his namesake, his missing uncle—everyone's favorite. Little did they know that this George would also leave them too soon.

Jim did very well at the Cumberland plant. Christmas Day, 1924 was a red-letter day: The first acetate yarn in the United States was spun at the plant on that day. Then in 1926, when Dad was eight and the family had spent two years in Maryland, Jim announced that the company was dispatching him to Quebec to help purchase and install the machinery for a new plant in Drummondville on the Saint-François River. The family was moving to Canada, and everyone packed up without complaint.

• • •

The family took pleasure in the four years they spent in Canada, although the early days dealing with another language were quite an experience. Hostility from the French Canadian kids was fierce. Gangs chased them down "like they wanted to murder us," Dad said. He and his friends were always careful to stay in groups of three or four "English."

The Celanese factory had a first-class soccer team, and Annie's brother, John Davidson—who'd also emigrated from Scotland to work for Celanese—was one of the best soccer players in all of Canada. The Elvins spent hours playing and watching soccer matches, and sometimes emotions ran high.

The family found the cold, biting winter in Drummondville exhilarating. Taxi drivers removed their tires and donned sled runners to cross the ice-bound river; Dad and his friends flew down the hills on toboggans at frightening speeds. My father loved living on the river and often hiked up to the falls above town. In April, huge chunks of ice—"as thick as a sofa," he remembered—would begin to give way on the Saint-François, an event that was met with great anticipation in town.

Later in the spring, they'd gather blueberries and Annie served up pies, jams, and cobblers. In the summer, they'd some-times latch onto the back of a farmer's horse and buggy. If the farmer wasn't in the mood for company, he'd send the whip back at them. Every summer, Dad and Georgie went off to Kamp Kanawana, a YMCA camp located on a remote lake in the Laurentians north of Montreal—one of what seemed to my father to be an endless series of thousands. The first time Georgie went, he was supposed to spend a week there but got so homesick he wouldn't stay. Dad stayed two weeks, improv-ing his swimming to the point where he finally made it across the lake. On the last day of camp, early in the morning, all the campers observed the camp ritual of jumping into the cool lake bare naked.

Each Sunday in Drummondville, they'd dress up for church. When they had first arrived in Canada, the family had attended the stately Episcopal church, but Jim said he couldn't put up with all that "bobbing up and down," and they helped to form a new branch of the United Church of Canada. Annie would sing both in the choir and at the church dinners that followed.

During the week, the children attended a school for "English" only. Walking by the French schools, Dad could hear the buzz of the children talking, but that wasn't the way in the English school, where they got whacked with a strap for talking in class. In fact, Dad got it once for being "smart." But school was so easy for him he almost considered it play. He remembered that the War of 1812 was taught decidedly in favor of the British, but after he returned to the United States, he heard the U.S. side of the story. In fact, Drummondville was established in 1815 to guard the Saint-François against U.S. attack and to provide a base for British soldiers.

Kay was always trying to keep up with the boys and she was so naturally athletic that she had little trouble doing so, while Georgie was always building and tinkering with things, and everyone knew he had Jim's innate talent for invention. Georgie was so much like Jim in that way that Annie often said he would inherit Jim's mantle of "engineer." Of course, Mary, the youngest, stayed close to home.

Dad and a friend often rode their bikes down to the train station to see the mighty Canadian National Railroad locomotives, said to be the largest the world had ever seen. Trains loomed large in Dad's memories of Drummondville. One day, news spread quickly that the railroad bridge had given way and the 4:13 train had plunged into the Saint-François. The engineer who bravely stayed at the throttle and brakes perished, but the fireman jumped and survived. No one else was killed.

The Great Depression was starting to hit Canada hard, and factories were reducing their workweeks because of declining exports. Every day, men came from all over to stand at the gates of the Celanese plant hoping for work, although the plant rarely hired anyone. Dad wondered how the men and their families survived.

•   •   •

In 1930, Jim told Celanese that he wanted to go back to either Maryland or Scotland, mainly because he didn't want his children educated in Catholic schools. They returned to Frostburg, but Dad missed Canada—the wilderness, the deep, sapphire-blue lakes, and the expanse of its open spaces. In Frostburg, he was thrown in with students who had spent their whole lives in or near the small mountain town, and some of them treated him roughly. Sports were so different in the States that he didn't have the faintest idea what to do on the track at school or in "football," played U.S. style.

My grandfather liked to tend his garden, and the family ate beets and potatoes year-round that he'd grown and stored under the house. He watched the weather carefully, recording it weekly in his diary. In May, he put in peas and beans; the tomatoes went into the ground in June. Fresh lettuce was plentiful in the spring and summer, and composted grass from the yard was used to fertilize the garden. The pear tree in the front yard and the grape arbor in the back meant fresh fruit in the summer and grape juice all winter.

The family didn't suffer unduly during the Depression, since Celanese was prospering. Jim and Annie had $300 in the First National Bank of Frostburg when it closed temporarily in 1933, but they eventually got back about 40 percent of what they had given up for lost.

Jim's diary occasionally noted not only the weather but church activities and the activities and accomplishments of his children. He sometimes included personal notes about the family in Scotland as well. The entry on February 26, 1931, indicates that he wrote to someone in Australia "about brother George." There's no record of a response to this latest effort to locate his brother, who'd now been missing for more than ten years.

Jim and Annie bought Dad a BB gun, and he put a target on the garage behind the house for practice. One day, the man from the house behind them came charging furiously across the yard. Dad had just missed shooting his wife in her rather ample rear end while she was scrubbing the floor on her hands and knees in the back of her house. Dad never used that target (either one) for shooting again, but the incident was dinner-table conversation at the Elvin home for months afterward.

In the early fall of 1932, Georgie became ill with rheumatic fever just as he was about to mark his twelfth birthday. Bill was fourteen at the time, and Kay and Mary were thirteen and seven, respectively.

Rheumatic fever was common among children in the early part of the twentieth century. It often developed about five weeks after a streptococcal (strep) throat infection. While it has no cure, rheumatic fever can now be prevented by treating strep throat with antibiotics—drugs that were either unknown or unavailable to doctors in Frostburg in 1932. Ironically, four years before Georgie took ill, biologist Alexander Fleming—a fellow Scotsman—had discovered penicillin. But it was not until 1943 that the required clinical trials were performed and mass production began, too late for George. Penicillin, of course, became widely available during World War II, and it was hailed as a medical miracle, saving thousands of soldiers, including my father, from the greatest wartime killer—infected wounds.

An inflammation developed in Georgie's heart when his body tried to fight the strep infection. In Jim's diary, the first reference to a problem with Georgie's health came in the entry for September 14, 1932, and from then on it got worse:

Took George to Dr. Cobey.

September 17: Dr. Cobey and Dr. Enfield held consultation on George's condition.

September 19: George taken to Memorial Hospital for XRay picture.

September 20: George's birthday. George given serum.

September 21: George given more serum.

September 22: George very ill. Given oxygen.

September 23: Stayed home. George very ill. Called in Dr. Bowen.

September 24: Stayed home.

September 25: George died.

As a child, I vividly remember passing by Georgie's picture as it sat on my grandmother's dresser—a little boy in shorts with sparkling dark eyes sitting on a chair too large for him, legs dangling, with a shock of black hair falling over his forehead. Often I would stop to look at it and wonder about him. When I asked Annie, her voice trembled and her eyes moistened. She just said, "That's my wee Georgie."

When the devastating news of Georgie's death reached friends and relatives, letters began to arrive from Scotland and Canada. Almost seventy years later, my father's voice broke with emotion over the phone when he told me about the letters. Annie's sister Charlotte wrote from Peterhead, "He was an awful kindly wee fellow. Mother spoke often of the children but I think oftenest of George. Words cannot express our sorrow." A telegram from Drummondville said, "Sorrow deeply with you all. Look up. It's all right." Robert Smith, the minister of the Presbyterian Church in Drummondville, wrote, "I can see the dear bright-eyed boy in the front chair by the centre isle looking up at me every Sunday morning."

Mary, the youngest child, was kept away from her brother during his illness—even from Kay and Bill. "Then one day," she said in a later interview with me:

> I was permitted to go into the room which had been off limits. There was Georgie in the casket and it was so sad to see. He'd been so full of zip and vinegar. He lay in that casket for several days. Then I was taken over to the Thomases, and I lived with them for a few more days while Mother tried to recoup. I had to go to school while everyone went to the funeral. That was very upsetting, but I'm sure Mother just felt she didn't need to be bothered with a seven-year-old. It felt so good when I could come home and we could all be together. But Bill became more serious after Georgie died—it made him grow up a little faster.

The funeral was held at the family home on Beall Street on a rainy Tuesday. Six members of Boy Scout Troop No. 1— twelve-year-olds dressed up in their neat uniforms—carried Georgie's small casket out of the house and down the walk and placed it gently in the hearse after the service. The other six troop members acted as flower bearers. Georgie was laid to rest in Frostburg Memorial Park, in a lovely spot on top of a hill overlooking the town.

But Georgie's death did nothing to shake my grandmother's deep religious faith. She found solace in her choir singing at church. There was always a hymn on her lips. At least once each day, as she went about her chores, she would sing "Abide With Me" in a clear, sweet voice, and its words comforted her: "Shine through the gloom and point me to the skies . . . In life, in death, O Lord, abide with me."

Jim recorded little in his diary for the next few months. The first entry after Georgie's death noted only "Rain showers. Democratic landslide—Roosevelt elected."

• • •

George Gardner, who went to high school with Dad, remembers when they both qualified to participate in a statewide track meet their senior year. After Gardner beat the state record in the "soccer kick," it was Dad's turn to see how far he could kick the ball. He immediately bested his friend's minutes-old record, then turned to him and apologized. That anecdote sums up my father's personality as well as anything: He couldn't help but excel—and he wanted to—but he was gracious in victory and a little uncomfortable showing up a friend.

The academic year at Beall High School included a declamation contest. Participants were to make a formal yet forceful speech about something. This was an event of importance, and it was well attended by the community. Dad ended up representing his school in the Allegany County finals, delivering a speech about the New Deal called "The War Today." The speech was an idealistic call for "a new kind of war" against economic inequality. Heir to Jim's intense compassion for working people and belief in their right to a decent life, Dad was always able to see beyond his own place in the world and empathize with people who were less fortunate.

To prepare for his oration, Dad's instructor had him stand on the stage in the combination auditorium/gymnasium. The instructor then coached him into a moderate but firm voice that could be clearly heard from the stage to the back wall. Many years later, Dad would echo his instructor, directing his children and grandchildren to "pro-JECT" their voices and "e-NUN-ciate" clearly. The drills gave him a confidence and ability that lasted throughout his lifetime. Later, at Fort Benning, as an officer candidate in the U.S. Army, he had no trouble with "Voice and Command."

After Georgie died, my father tried to fill the "engineer"

slot left vacant by his brother's death and to replace the hole left in the family the only way he knew how. Encouraged by of one of his teachers, Dad applied to and was accepted by the Massachusetts Institute of Technology (MIT). But the teacher later thought Dad might not want to stay with engineering and recommended he also apply to the University of Michigan, where he could transfer to another major if he wished. My father entered the University of Michigan in 1936, majoring in engineering, and the teacher turned out to be right—by the end of his first year in college, Dad found himself much more engrossed in his courses in English, political science, and economics. He discovered Sinclair Lewis, and before the end of the year he'd read more than a dozen of his novels. Lewis, the first American to win the Pulitzer Prize for Literature, was known for his concern with issues of race, women, and the powerless in society, as exemplified by his novels such as *Main Street*, *Babbitt*, and *Arrowsmith*. Some called him the conscience of his generation, and he made the famous statement that "when fascism comes to America, it will be wrapped in the flag and carrying a cross."

My father became the associate editor of the respected *Michigan Daily*, the university newspaper. The *Daily* staff was roughly divided between the status quo group, who generally rooted for the university and its glory, and the dissatisfied group, who were leftist or liberal (more along Dad's line, I suspect). The distinction between the two was not always clear, however. The liberal group was all for free speech until the right-wing extremist Father Charles Coughlin—whose weekly radio broadcasts reached 40 million Americans and vilified Roosevelt's New Deal and "Jewish conspirators" while praising Hitler and Mussolini—was silenced by his bishop. Then they were quite pleased that the "voice of discord" had been "stilled," as the *Detroit Free Press* put it.

Writing for a newspaper became my father's passionate ambition. When Edward R. Murrow, one of the greatest figures in the history of American journalism, came to Ann Arbor to deliver a lecture, Dad made sure he spoke with him and asked his advice: To prepare for a career as a newspaperman, should he change his major from history-economics to journalism? Murrow told him to stick with the history and economics because a knowledge and understanding of the world was more important for a journalist to master than journalism courses. Meeting Murrow was a landmark in my father's career path, and he followed Murrow's example of clean, straightforward, well-written reporting like a beacon for the rest of his writing life.

According to my father, his parents took the news of his change in career path well enough. They wanted him to be happy first and foremost, but to my "up-by-the-bootstraps" grandfather, reporting for a newspaper must have looked like a shaky basis for a livelihood.

My uncle Frank Dwyer, Kay's husband, disputes Dad's view that his parents approved of his change in direction. "I have a picture in my mind of Bill and Jim," Uncle Frank recalled, "standing on the front porch trying to communicate their differences without having a confrontation. Bill is standing with arms folded and so is Jim. They are both facing forward, neither looking at the other. Jim wanted to convince Bill the way to go, wanted him to be an engineer."

Kay and Frank dated while in college at the University of Maryland, and Frank went to visit her at the Elvin home in Frostburg one Thanksgiving. He had only met her older brother, Bill, once before. Even then he sensed some competition between them. The temperature in Frostburg was well below freezing that day, and Kay—ever the adventuress—wanted to go sledding, but because Frank's clothes weren't warm enough, she loaned him a pair of Jim's trousers. Afterward, he wound up pulling Kay on the sled back to the house. As Frank recalled it, "Bill comes out of the door, tearing by us on his way somewhere, and he calls out, 'Dwyer, your fly's open!' "

As graduation from the University of Michigan approached, Dad sent letters to as many as sixty newspapers seeking employment. A few replied, most of them with rejections. The Depression was beginning to ease, but jobs were still hard to find. Publishers at the *Cumberland News and Times*, the *Baltimore Sun*, the *Washington Post*, and the *Washington Evening Star* had a backlog of good applicants. An application to the Celanese plant landed Dad a job in the personnel office for $125 a month, but he found it depressing to be constantly telling applicants that there was no work for them.

•   •   •

On a trip to the University of Maryland to visit Kay, Dad met her friend Jane Legge. Dark-haired, pretty, and vivacious, she had an outgoing and upbeat personality that was the perfect complement to his more serious bent. Jane was from Cumberland, just down the road from Frostburg. Her father was an attorney in Cumberland and had served as mayor several years before. Her mother was a schoolteacher who also volunteered for the Red Cross and other charities. Jane was majoring in English and planned to attend graduate school at the University of Pennsylvania School of Social Work, but my father told her he didn't want his wife to work. Mom said later that that's actually how he proposed to her, saying "I don't want my wife to work." It was hardly the romantic scene she'd envisioned all her life.

But by all accounts, they were very much in love and were married on November 1, 1941. While they treasured their newlywed status like any other couple, dancing cheek-to-cheek to "Stardust" and sending sweet cards and notes to each other, they already worried that U.S. entry into World War II (which had begun in Europe in 1939) was imminent. They knew that they could soon be separated. When the Japanese attacked Pearl Harbor on December 7, and the United States entered the war soon after, they knew that they were right.

Mrs. Eisenberger, the wife of the Presbyterian minister in Cumberland, urged Dad to register as a conscientious objector and told his mother as much. Annie wished he could go that route, but she knew he would never agree. Instead, he wanted to volunteer for Officer Candidate School but was surprised to learn that he was not eligible because he wasn't a citizen. He thought that when his parents became citizens, he'd automatically become one, too. But it turned out that since he was over eighteen years of age, he was not covered and had to start the whole process from scratch at twenty-four years old. He had no trouble qualifying for Officer Candidate School once the citizenship requirement was met. He was a college graduate, and he'd attained a Grade I score on the Army General Classification Test, a test of intelligence.

In September 1942, he reported to Fort Meade, Maryland. He immediately got night duty washing huge pots and pans, but after someone found out that he could type, he spent three weeks in an office on the base before being sent to Camp Croft near Spartanburg, South Carolina. My mother joined him and they celebrated their second Christmas together in Spartanburg. But when he went to Fort Benning in Columbus, Georgia for Officer Training School in January of 1943, Mom went back to Cumberland. The seventeen-week course at Fort Benning was grueling at times: bayonet exercise, hiking with a full field pack, rifle instruction, and worst of all, the obstacle courses. What made it different was that only a third of the candidates would become officers; the rest would be shipped off to fill the enlisted ranks of infantry divisions. Strong vocal skills were crucial, since more candidates failed because of "lack of force and aggressiveness" than anything else. They were also under constant observation, not only from the officers and instructors but also from each other, and were required to fill out confidential forms rating their peers' potential as combat officers.

April 14, 1943 brought Dad happy news of the birth of his first child, a son named after him, William John Elvin—nicknamed "Jay." He sent my mother a telegram that day: "Wonderful, honey, say hello to Jay for me waiting to hear all about everything love Bill."

By the end of April my father was assigned to the 35th Officer Replacement Battalion at Camp Croft. Mom and Jay joined him again until he was transferred to Camp Breckenridge, Kentucky, just before D-Day. All too soon it was time for First Lieutenant Elvin to go to war. Returning to Cumberland on July 6, 1944, he and my mother stayed in the Commodore Hotel for one last night together (at a cost of $6.93) before he shipped out.

Mary, then eighteen, remembers the family seeing Dad off to Europe that summer. "I can still see the train station in Cumberland, and Bill so handsome in his uniform. He kissed us all, and then he kissed his wife goodbye." She thought it was all so romantic.

The train station was abuzz with the nervousness and excitement of all the soldiers and their families who had gathered to say farewell. While tearful and anxious, most managed to put on brave faces. My mother held Jay in her arms as she stood on tiptoe to kiss her soldier goodbye. The unknown future stretched out like tracks of the train that was headed far from the hills of Western Maryland.

CHAPTER THREE

Life in the Foxhole

"In combat, there's acid dripping in your stomach,
droplet by droplet, even in the good times."
—Tim O'Brien, Vietnam veteran and writer, in an NPR interview

The Moselle River was one of the last great barriers before the Siegfried Line, a powerful system of concrete and steel fortifications set up by the Germans along their western frontier in World War I. During World War II, the German Army knew how to defend a river crossing and had no intention of easily giving up its hold on the Moselle. The United Press reported in September of 1944 that German troops lining the rain-swept river had received orders to "fight to the last man" so as to give other forces time to take up positions along the Siegfried Line. After all, they were getting close to home: The German border was now a scant fifty miles away.

From early September and into November 1944, the 80th Infantry Division of Patton's Third Army crossed the Moselle at various points, mounting an effort some historians say had no parallel in U.S. military history since Ulysses S. Grant's army struggled to cross the Mississippi and strike at Vicksburg in 1863. American troops fought hard and succeeded in opening a hole for the tanks of the 4th Armored Division to come through in mid-September, followed by more infantry. The infantry marched from one village to the next—Ste. Genevieve, Ville-au-Val, Loisy, Landremont, Autreville. They attacked hill after hill, enduring scorching and deafening enemy artillery, often to be turned back.

The Americans and the Germans were battling over the area of Ste. Genevieve Ridge, a long, kidney-shaped hill running north and south. The small village of Ste. Genevieve rested at the north end of the hill. By late afternoon on September 13, the village of Ste. Genevieve had changed hands several times. Now, as many as six German battalions had regrouped and pushed back determinedly toward Dieulouard, breaking through roadblocks put up by the 2nd Battalion, 318th Regiment.

After Lieutenant Blanchard, my father, and several others had gotten separated from E Company, they headed back across the bridge to Dieulouard. My father's journal continued:

We still had troops across the Moselle and tanks were lined up back in Dieulouard ready to come up and across. We decided to go back to Dieulouard, round up as many men as we could, and get back up on the hill. Dieulouard was still being shelled, so every once in a while we had to duck into a building. We had told every man we wanted that the Aid Station would be the assembly point; it was not a good choice. The lightly wounded were almost cheerful but there were others you did not like to see when you knew you were going right back up the hill.

The supply sergeant gave us two jeeps to relay the men over and we made our way through traffic jams and artillery barrages to the hill. Blanchard and I kept inquiring for E Company. We reached Ste. Genevieve, and Company G of the 317th was at the top of the hill. Hell, no, they hadn't seen E-318. G-317 was rounding up prisoners, so we helped them.

We fired into houses and hollered, and prisoners came out with their hands up.

We came to the edge of Ste. Genevieve, looking down into the valley across our hill from the Moselle. We beheld a remarkable and fascinating sight. Below us stretched the long, wide valley, lovely and peaceful in the sunshine, and weaving its way down a bright brown road was the 4th Armored, their pink-red identification panels glistening in the sun. They were moving, slowly, like good soldiers, keeping good distance. It looked as though the war might be over; the armor was rolling far into the distance and nothing was trying to stop it.

Our fascination was interrupted by a sound up on the hillside to our right; we saw something move. I suggested that someone go up and take a look, but nobody moved. I went up and one man came with me; there were GIs, remnants of a company that had had a rough time the night before. They knew nothing of E-318's whereabouts.

On the road in front of us was a mashed Kraut. Every tank had made an effort to go around him but he was right in the middle of the little road.

Farther down, on the road from Bezaumont to the river highway, was a Nazi tank, knocked out. The crew had tried to escape and hadn't made it. In the ditches were dead Krauts. They never let dead GIs lie around.

Soon we ran right into E Company and there was a great exchanging of stories.

September 14, 1944, Ville-au-Val—E Company was protecting and securing its Battalion Command Post and its roadblock near Autreville.

I saw Graham; he told me he thought the Germans were back in Ville-au-Val, although Carr of E-318 had taken a patrol through there without difficulty.

*We were very much exposed and the ground was like iron.
My shovel bent like wax but after hours of brutal work I had a
satisfactory hole dug. Just then a runner came up, in the rain,
to tell us we were to move out immediately.*

*The new position was not far away, and the ground was just
as bad there. All the men were naturally in a bad humor and
the rain kept pouring down. Three times the order came down,
from man to man, to get ready to move out, but each time the
order was countermanded. We were all cold and filthy, and still
it rained. The weapons were in bad shape but it wasn't necessary
to tell anyone to start cleaning; we all knew that a failure to fire
might cost us heavily.*

*In the morning we moved up the slope [the high ground at
Mousson Hill]. We were right out in the open. As the day
wore on, it became clear that the Germans had let the 4th
Armored come through them and now were counterattacking
us very heavily all around the perimeter of our bridgehead.
The men became increasingly bitter and agitated as the day
wore on.*

September 14–16, 1944, Loisy—The German Panzers (tanks)
continued their fierce counterattacks and the soggy, wet
weather persisted. The 318th's immediate goal was the high
ground of Mousson Hill, key to maintaining the bridgehead at
the river. They reached it but couldn't consolidate their position, and the Germans counterattacked, pounding their armor
against the GI's.

*About five o'clock I got a call to go back to the Company
Command Post. The Captain was very much concerned, telling
me, "Everything is pulling back across the river; the Jerries are
coming in on every side and before long they'll be in front of
your position. I'm sending you forty replacements; get them dug
in with good fields of fire. Keep everybody on alert. And, we lost*

White today." [Lieutenant Willie White was one of the officers who had come in the previous week, along with Blanchard, Carr, and Santner.]

The replacements were waiting when I got back to the platoon. It was getting dark and I didn't have time to tell each of them more than, "Sergeant Garza is in charge of your squad. Dig in here, fast. We're expecting trouble."

One new soldier stopped me cold by insisting he wanted to know what was going on before I went on down the line. He reminded me of Camp Croft and maneuvers; I almost laughed. But his question did make me realize how the situation must look to the new men, and I made it a point after that to talk a little bit as I moved along.

After the digging was well under way, I went around and arranged the guard for the night. There were two men in each hole—a suggestion of the Major's that worked very well. Both men in a hole were to sleep at the same time, with the men on either side awake. The night was absolutely quiet, and the soupy dawn arrived with a gentleness and assurance that changed every man from a fearsome, groveling worm to a warm, self-respecting human being.

The next afternoon brought a spectacle, a front row seat at battle. With his field glasses, my father scanned the landscape all around and saw the frightful battle over in Loisy, where the Germans had chosen to make another big push.

Over on the far left, toward Loisy, a terrific battle was going on. Apparently the Jerries had chosen that flank, rather than ours, for the big push. The machine gun near Bezaumont kept firing . . . hubahubahubahubahub. Apparently the gunner had a good hole; we couldn't see him although we could plainly see the gun. One of our tanks moved along the ridge at the top of a hill. He got just beyond the machine gun when the artillery started breaking around him. He twisted and turned but still it came and how they missed him was a miracle. Finally, he ducked into what seemed like pathetically little cover. We waited. The next round seemed to be a hit. The tank never moved again and the machine gun was quiet.

Jerry didn't have our artillery spotted because their replies landed among a group of horses on the hill below Bezaumont. You could hear comments on all sides about the horses being hurt; the men were having the war and somehow it was more piteous for the animals to be wounded. All around us were cows that had been caught by the artillery, lying in grotesque positions.

Up on the ridge above where the tank had been knocked out we saw men moving around. Some of the sharp-eyed, using the field glasses, said they were definitely GIs. Somebody said they'll catch it for showing themselves on the skyline; they did, and raced around like ants looking for cover.

The sky was clear and bright and we looked for the P-47s [fighter planes]. The possibility of their arrival—always hoped for about four in the afternoon—was still being discussed when someone shouted and pointed.

There they were, beautiful, beautiful, high in the sky and looking for trouble. Every upturned face was held in a kind of ecstasy. It's not just the actual physical help that they bring, it's being remembered and knowing that you're part of a mighty war machine.

They zoomed in on Jerry, spraying like mad. Jerry got two of them; the pilots bailed out and the planes landed and burst into flames. We watched the pilots parachuting far to our left and hoped they would land in friendly territory.

Every eye watched the rest of the planes head for home and you'd have thought every man was watching his love walk away after tender parting.

The foggy morning of September 15 saw the largest German counterattack yet. The town of Atton, at the foot of Mousson Hill, was nearly destroyed. Ste. Genevieve and Hill 382 changed hands several times as casualties mounted. E Company kept clawing its way up the hill, only to be stopped often by terrible barrages of artillery fire.

> *I hadn't been feeling well; I moved away from our new line of foxholes and was miserably sick. The Major told me to get the company ready to move down the river to Loisy and Atton, where we would have to post defense against a threatened counterattack. Loisy was quiet. About 50 yards down the road, we had to hit the ditches. The wrong party knew we were coming. His shells were landing just below us on the side of the road. Several times I started to get up and get things going again but Jerry kept pelting us. Morale was at a new low as we dragged into Atton. The Captain met me and said there might be Jerry tanks heading our way but that we didn't have any of our own.*
>
> *During the night the Jerries shelled our position. The first few rounds were just over but then one landed in our field and we could hear the brrrbmmmmwhuuuung of flying shrapnel. In the morning I was sick again and didn't eat. Most of the men were sick, too. I took a walk through the battered, still-burning village [Atton]. I checked in at the Command Post and found things in that I-don't-know-and-who-gives-a-damn state of affairs.*

They were in motion constantly now, from town to town, hill to hill.

> *In the afternoon we got orders to move again: back to The Hill [Mousson] and Bezaumont, but we had tanks and tank destroyers now. The night was bitterly cold. But Jerry didn't*

make a sound. In the morning, we moved again, this time south toward Autreville. One of the men almost got us disorganized when his rifle discharged accidentally. I left a medic with him and passed word on up the line that everything was all right. The word almost certainly never got all the way up. I know of no message not obvious to everyone that was passed up to the head of any column larger than a squad.

The next day I set a moderate pace, thinking of the men in the rear, especially those carrying weapons. But after awhile the first sergeant sent word would I please speed up, artillery was falling back of them.

In the morning we moved to the left, to the top of the ridge. The 317th had been occupying an old World War I trench that ran along the crest. The men we were relieving looked like inhabitants of a ghost town; they were far beyond fatigue and just this side of unconsciousness.

The next day we were on the road again, almost to Ste. Genevieve. We got a day's rest, and the countryside was beautiful. The sun came out; the grapevines were heavy. For the first time in three weeks I wrote letters and shaved.

The 80th had secured the bridgeheads at the Moselle at last. Now the battle shifted eastward, toward the River Seille. But Patton's mad dash from Normandy toward Germany had slowed to a standstill. The Division was to move only twenty miles in the next two months.

SEPTEMBER 17, 1944—We moved out again on a long march to Ville-au-Val; I was so sick now and had tried doing and not doing so many things that nothing seemed to make any difference. We had three days' K-rations. In addition, I had cigarettes in every pocket; a carbine magazine in my carbine, four in my pistol belt, and several more in my pockets. Also a flashlight, candle, carbine cleaning equipment, water purification tablets, a wool knitted cap, insignia, matches, gloves, a half-blanket, shovel, trench-knife, first aid packet, grenades, letters, and pictures.

There was a hell of a fight going on just up the hill in front of us. We stood around or leaned against a tree or sat down, not saying a word. Waiting. A leaf would fall from a tree and every man would start and look at his buddy. Up front someone would shout something indistinct; in a hoarse whisper, coated with fear, a rifleman would ask a mortarman, "What was that?" And the answer would always be a dull, "I dunno."

By this time we had had enough. "Watch where you're wavin' your damn M-1." Ambulances and stretcher-bearers went by in a steady stream. Worried-looking officers hurried back and forth. I checked with the officers up ahead; things were not going well and were all fouled up.

First and 3rd platoons were in the lead, I was with the 2nd Weapons Platoon, in support. We twisted our way through the brush. There was firing of small arms, including a Jerry machine gun. Suddenly everything was confusion and some of the men from the 1st and 3rd platoons started running through us. We had heavy machine guns set up and on the order of the attached heavy weapons officer they prepared to fire.

Men were all ganged up around the guns; I told them to spread out. The sound of their footsteps and thrashings hadn't died away when the air was rent with the most doom-laden crack I had ever heard. It was like the crack that burning wood makes, but a thousand times louder and right in front of your face.

This time there was a mass exodus from the immediate area; we were in for it now. The crew of one of the machine guns had been wiped out and a number of other men had been wounded.

I found Carr and Santner who were both trying to salvage the situation. Not a man from the Weapons Platoon had taken off; I told them later how much I thought of them for that. I then told them to move back 50 yards and spread out.

My runner had two Krauts, who said there were 26 more just over there. They wanted to surrender but they had a newly-commissioned officer who wouldn't let them. We had them carry our most seriously wounded to the rear and they were cravenly obliging.

During the night I was sick, so sick I thought I would never feel well again. About three o'clock in the morning there was a terrific mortar barrage that landed some 300 yards away. Jerry didn't fire again but we stayed awake because of our poor position.

On top of the hill, vehicles were moving. Artillery barrages were murderous and almost continuous. Word came back that a man up front had just been killed by a sniper; keep a sharp lookout to the right. The next barrage was close and we knew we were moving into the area of concentration. Every face was a death mask.

We moved along Bratte Hill, most of it heavily wooded, with the great fields of the Sivry Valley on our left. We took a position on a nose of the hill overlooking the valley. We were ahead of our own riflemen and other companies were at our rear. Dusk was just beginning to set in when we saw what appeared to be a company of our troops move out of Bratte, to our left, in attack formation. They were heading for Sivry; their entire route along the valley was over open ground.

The company moved across our front; they were having no trouble at all. Apparently the Germans knew that they were outflanked and had pulled out of Sivry, which was between us and the Moselle.

But suddenly the slowly moving men stopped; it was like a

motion picture that stopped unaccountably, presenting a strange still shot. Then we, too, heard the wheeeeeeng, saw the horrible black bursts, and heard the CALACK! CALACK! CALACK! The soldiers ran for cover but there was none except what looked like the bed of a very small stream.

Then the Jerry machine guns in the edge of Sivry opened up, moving back and forth. The men were pushing forward again, knowing that their only hope was to get into the town. Another barrage stormed in on them.

Meanwhile, we were scanning Sivry for possible targets. Suddenly all of us shouted at the same time; at the corner of a house was smoke from the muzzle blast of a gun.

Immediately the men wanted to fire; I said no. Our position, as far as we knew, was still unknown to the enemy and our orders were restricted to firing on targets on the Sivry road. The shrapnel hummed and sang all over the field. One of our brace heavy machine guns was silenced. Again the Jerry barked.

But his position was unmistakably clear now And when the men looked at me again, I said go ahead. We couldn't see our first two mortar rounds but the third looked like a direct hit. Our gunner was beside himself with joy. We used his range and started laying stuff in all along the edge of Sivry.

A runner came up with a message that I was to cease firing immediately. The attack had collapsed and the men who were able were making their way back to Bratte. In a very few minutes there was a great SWISH! Right over our heads and a huge explosion on the hill just behind us. Some huge gun had turned around to show us that we had better behave; then he had gone about his business.

Just after breakfast the next morning, the Jerries moved in right over our heads. I moved the men off into the woods and joined the rest of the company. We were joined by another company in a counterattack at very close range—50 to 100 yards. We inched along, firing when we stopped. The din was deafening. Machine guns were blazing away at each other. It seemed that a fight of such intensity couldn't go on very long.

The firing became savage, but in a few minutes it was over. There were dead and wounded all around. When we got up to the Kraut positions, we found their bodies. They were poor-looking, a far cry from super-men, and their weapons didn't seem a match for ours, rifle for rifle, machine gun for machine gun.

September 24, 1944—The order came for Easy (E) Company to prepare to move to Mount St. Jean. Fox (F) Company had been up there, cut off for several days. The roads were so rain-soaked as to be nearly impassable.

Fox Company had taken a terrific beating but was still there. I asked the Captain of Fox Company about Graham; he said Graham had been hit and evacuated. No one seemed sure of what had happened to him, but I found out later that he had been observing artillery when a piece of shrapnel tore into the side of his head. I saw him later in England, just before he went back to the States.

One of the stories Dad told us about the war was about his friend Norval Graham. A member of F Company, which lost more than half of its members, Graham was sent home. He went to see my grandmother. When Annie saw the young man she'd known for years standing on her front porch, she nearly fainted. His disfiguring head wound frightened her.

At 7 A.M., the 2nd Battalion of the 318th attacked Mount St. Jean. The sun had begun to shine but Mount St. Jean, which was higher than the other hills, was very muddy and slippery. They reached the woods past the second plateau but were stopped after so many men were wounded by hostile fire. During this attack, a battalion of the 317th moved to the first plateau to protect the rear and right flank of the 318th's 2nd Battalion. Directly in front of them in a narrow clearing, mounds of World War I gun emplacements rose at regular intervals. Dad said later, "Sometimes we were in WWI emplacements but the Germans had us zeroed in. They'd start firing at you and then their observer would say, well that was too short, too long, too far to the right or left. Finally, they'd find you. They just about destroyed our outfit."

> *My runner had been killed. Another man who had been assigned to the company through typographical error—he was supposed to go to C Company, I believe—had been killed.*
>
> *Blanchard was to lead the attack with his rifle platoon. They moved forward about 25 yards before they received heavy small arms fire from the direct front. Just at that point, amazingly enough, there was a substantial ditch running across his position. Several men were unable to make it to the ditch.*
>
> *Blanchard was doing a good job. He would shout, "When I fire we all fire!" and every man would let go a few rounds before taking cover again.*

Lieutenant Gene Blanchard wrote to his parents to fill them in on his fellow officers. "There's Lieutenant Elvin," he wrote, "who I fight with all the time. Just in fun, but we argue every chance we get. He is a hard worker and very conscientious."

Blanchard, my father, and the other first lieutenants led their platoons on patrols into the woods. The platoon (consisting of approximately forty men) would set off in a certain direction, but it was often difficult to know which way to go, as combat produced chaos and desperate confusion. Messengers ran between units in the midst of artillery fire and the evacuation of men who'd been maimed or killed. And sometimes in the dark, while the enemy couldn't be seen, their horses could be heard approaching like ghosts in the night.

Many night patrols, of five to fifteen men, out of E Company were led by Lieutenant Walter Carr. He was so successful at bringing back information about enemy strength and position that he became known as the "night patrol man." Sometimes he would obtain the information by scouting visually, sometimes by capturing a prisoner who would then talk. He'd earned a reputation as a totally reliable patrol leader. Carr told me my father had a lot of confidence and took the initiative. "Your father was a replacement officer, like me, but he was promoted in the States before I was. He had rank over me, but I knew that immediately, they didn't even have to tell me. He'd go right in where all hell was breaking loose."

Lieutenant Carr was modest about his own feats. He did not mention to me that he had earned two Silver Stars for gallantry in action, led more patrols than anyone else, and been wounded three times. In addition, during the Battle of the Bulge, leading a four-man patrol, he stole through German lines into Bastogne to contact the trapped 101st Airborne. In spite of remarkable achievements like these, Carr illustrates the almost universal modesty one sees from the brave soldiers of this era.

• • •

The men would scramble for the protection of the trenches as the ground burst into flame from artillery shelling. In *Citizen Soldiers*, Stephen Ambrose cites Captain John Colby, who was amazed to see how small he could make his body during artillery fire. If you got caught in a shelling, Colby advised, "the best thing to do is drop to the ground and crawl into your steel helmet. One's body tends to shrink a great deal when shells come in. I am sure I have gotten as much as 80 percent of my body under my helmet when caught in shellfire."[1]

The 2nd and 3rd Battalions tried again, unsuccessfully, to take Mount St. Jean. According to the *After Action Report*, they were "stopped again with heavy losses." Then, on September 25, 1944, orders came for a coordinated attack by F and G Companies, with E in reserve, across open terrain, on Mount Toulon, Mount St. Jean, and the high ground overlooking the Seille River near Benicourt, Clemery, and Manoncourt.

We were in an uncomfortable position, but there was an exhilaration in a small arms fire that was far removed from the cringing terror of an artillery barrage. The months at Fort Benning and Camp Croft had given me a little confidence about this sort of thing.

But the artillery barrage resumed. The Germans emptied their weapons, covering the valley with ferocious automatic weapon crossfire and barrages of mortar and artillery.

Blanchard was hollering for mortars; I asked him what he could see for me to fire at. He said, "Hell's fire! You know they're out there!"

Just then, a voice just to my left said, "Don't move, Lootenant, there's a Jerry with a grenade about 15 yards ahead of you." The soldier took careful aim and fired. "OK, Lootenant."

The next day we shoved off again, but were stopped cold. We were definitely going to get some attention. The German mortars were practicing, shifting here and there along our position. They had excellent observation from the village down to our right.

The enemy was zeroing in on E Company. The sky was exploding.

The mortars started bracketing our position. We moved back about 50 yards; then the mortars fell behind us, so we decided to move back half the distance we had come. We were all on our feet when a barrage landed. Two men were wounded in the arms and legs. Four of the men formed a carrying party to take them to the rear. That was one of the details officers never caught—helping the wounded to the rear and taking prisoners back.

We were all worn out. There was no chatter at all. Nerves were on edge. There was a rumor that we were going to be relieved but even that rumor was tossed around bitterly. If they don't get us out of here soon, there won't be anything left to relieve.

On Mount St. Jean, progress was no better. Fox Company also had been stopped cold. Late in the afternoon of September 26, rations were brought up. The men went back to their emplacements and were in all sorts of positions when the next barrage landed. Some were badly hurt.

Our emplacement would be next. We heard the sound more clearly than ever before: pop, pop, pop. Three mortar rounds were on the way, and we knew their destination.

Not since the first night across the Moselle when the artillery was crashing in had I felt with such certainty that this was the end. Half our men were gone, and the rest were going. So the rounds were on the way; nothing could stop them. Those who escape the shrapnel will get the concussion.

We heard the whirring swish . . . the gods were playing badminton. Our bodies were so tense that it seemed impossible that they could tighten more, but they did. Tight, tight, tight, and down, down, down.

The first round landed right over our heads about two feet from the edge of the emplacement. Whirrrrswwwish! And the second landed so close to the edge that we got dirt all over us. Whirrrrrswwwwish! The third landed just to the right.

One of the men wounded in the first barrage had been a

runner who was coming down to tell us we were going to be relieved. The men were in a rebellious frame of mind because we had to stay until the final order came. The wounded were moaning. The rain kept coming down. The men kept coming up to me and asking when we were going to move; they were sweating out every minute on that hill.

Still, they advanced slowly through the mud and the rain. (Some soldiers said there's no mud in the world as sticky, deep, or wet as European mud.) But with the aid of gun and mortar fire of H Company, they finally managed to reach the high ground of Mount St. Jean.

Sometime during the night we heard GI voices; it was the 317th. An officer came up and I told him what had been going on. He was tired and unshaven and wanted to rest. Suddenly he put his hand on my arm and said, "For Christ's sake, Elvin." It was Frank Congelosi, who had come all the way from Fort Meade to the 80th with Ellsworth, Graham, and me. We had a quiet laugh over the changes a few weeks had brought.

We moved back behind the line of emplacements and still we were not relieved. The men were more unfriendly to me than they had ever been before. I lay down in the water and slept until the first faint dawn.

The next day, an anti-aircraft battery to our left caught a barrage. There was no doubt the Krauts had observation, and morale dropped to a new low.

Sometime in the night it started again. The shell-bursts were terrific, not the mortar explosions we had had on our side of Mount St. Jean. A vicious barrage landed to our front, momentarily lighting up our position. Then more. And more. And more. To the right. To the left. Right behind. It was never going to stop.

I lay down in my foxhole and hoped the next round would hit me right square on the head.

NOTE

1. Stephen E. Ambrose, *Citizen Soldiers: The U.S. Army from the Normandy Beaches to the Bulge to the Surrender of Germany, June 7, 1944, to May 7, 1945* (New York: Simon & Schuster, 1997), p. 46.

CHAPTER FOUR

"Don't Surprise Your Father"

"Tight, tight, tight, and down, down, down."
—Dad's journal, France, September 1944

"If you wake your father when he's napping on the couch, do it from across the room," my mother warned. As we learned, our usually unflappable father could inadvertently become violent. The rules were clear: Never sneak up behind him and never disturb his sleep. "I'm not responsible for what I do if you do that," he'd say. Jumping on Daddy's back, the way most kids do, was out of the question. Although he didn't want to hurt us, his reaction would be automatic.

Even as an adult I found waking him a nerve-wracking experience. After I'd married and had a child, Dad and I lived only ten miles apart, so we frequently visited back and forth. One day when Dad came for lunch, we planned to pick up my son from school, but in the meantime Dad got tired and stretched out on the couch. The October afternoon sun warmed the living room as he napped. When three o'clock arrived, he was still asleep, and I began to get nervous.

Standing across the room, my palms sweated as I tried to decide what to do. The clock was ticking, and the air felt warm and sticky. I grabbed a broom, feeling like a little girl sneaking up on an unpredictable giant. Tiptoeing over to the couch, I prodded him gently in the back with the broom. Immediately, he shot up like a fish jumping out of the water. "What? What's going on?"

"Daddy, we have to go get Ben. Are you awake?"

He sat up, looked at me, focusing now, and sighed. He smoothed his thick, slightly graying hair and put his glasses back on. Standing to his full six feet, he said, "All right, then, let's get this show on the road." I wiped my moist palms on my pants and we headed out the door.

• • •

For as long as I can remember, the sound of a thunderclap, the noise of a car backfiring, or the roar of an airplane overhead would startle my father. The first report of this came in early 1946 when he, my mother, and my brother Jay lived below the flight path to Washington's National Airport. At night, when he awoke to the sound of the planes coming in low, Dad would throw my mother off the bed onto the floor, diving on her to protect her from an aerial attack. He also struck out in his sleep, sometimes accidentally hitting my mother. She often had to wake him from a nightmare, and when she did, he awoke with a jolt, ready to "return fire."

The great war correspondent Ernie Pyle wrote about noise, lightning, and thunder in a front-line dispatch from France in 1944. Describing the effect of a thunderstorm on combat troops, he said:

> Last night we had a violent electrical storm around our
> countryside. The storm was half over before we realized that
> the flashes and crashings around us were not artillery but plain
> old-fashioned thunder and lightning. It will be odd to hear only
> thunder again. You must remember that such things as that are
> in our souls, and will take time.[1]

Dad hardly spoke about what he had seen and done overseas, and when he did, it was more about the mechanics of it than the feelings. Dad's sister Mary later said, "It was like pulling teeth to get him to talk about the war."

While my father fought overseas, Jay and my mother lived with her parents in Cumberland, Maryland, with Dad's family close by in Frostburg. Jay was doted on by his mother, two aunts, and two sets of first-time grandparents. Dad's return disrupted his young life, bringing in a stranger and authority figure from out of the blue. After World War II, thousands of fathers came back to children who were strangers to them, but that made it no less painful to my brother. Dad's homecoming burst the three-year-old's cocoon. At Jay's initial glimpse of his father coming up the walk, he cried, "Shoo-scram-de-bullet-de-bingbong-de-galloping-horse—go *away*, you snake-in-the-grass!" And later, a plaintive, "Do I have to mind you, too?"

He saw his idyllic life torn asunder when Dad returned. Under the best of circumstances, Jay's life since childhood has not been easy, marred by alcoholism and depression (now under control, for which he gives credit to AA), and I know that he attributes some of his problems to our father.

The new threesome of mother, father, and son barely had time to bond before I was born in late 1946, at the front end of the postwar generation known as the baby boomers. Just before my arrival, the family moved to the northern Virginia area, but our ties to Western Maryland remained strong. We visited and vacationed there often.

In fact, a photo taken of Dad and me on a family vacation at Deep Creek Lake in Oakland, Maryland, captures one of my favorite memories of him. I was three years old when the photograph was taken in 1949; Dad is kneeling beside me helping me fish off a pier with a stick and a piece of string. With his good looks and my blond hair, we look like JFK and Caroline.

In that moment, I was well-protected from toddling off into the water by my father's arm close around me and a life vest. I love the picture because I was wearing my little red tennis shoes, which I adored as only a little girl can adore red shoes. One of them fell off the pier that day into the water, and I was heartbroken.

"I'll get it. Watch!" said Dad, as the rest of the family laughed. He looked at me and gestured for me to give him the other shoe. When I did, he dropped my remaining shoe into the lake—and dove in after it. I stared down at the water under which he'd nearly disappeared, and my heart sank along with the shoe. What was he doing? How would he ever find both of them in the murky water of the lake? Then, miraculously, he popped up with a splash, holding one red shoe in each hand. After he'd pulled himself back onto the pier, we all demanded to know, "How'd you *do* that?" He stood up and, as the sun shone on him, seemed tremendous as I looked up at him with big eyes. Tennis shoe number two led him to tennis shoe number one, he said. I didn't know how he'd done it, but one thing was sure: To my three-year-old mind, my dad could do magic.

In our family, the Army was always a presence, especially in the early days of my childhood. After *The Howdy Doody Show* ended and Mom was about to put dinner on the table, Dad would unleash the pidgin German he'd learned during the war. We found it vastly entertaining when he would bark, "Vashender handender hoak!"—his mishmash of "Wash your hands" and "Hands up!" If he wanted us to leave the room he'd say, "Rausmitsche"—"Get out!"

He taught us to sing the fight songs from both their colleges, Michigan and Maryland, and best of all, "The Infantry Song." We liked "The Infantry Song" because it said the infantry had dirt behind their ears. We sang these songs hundreds of times on long car rides, mostly to visit family in neighboring states. Jay and I played all the usual car games on these trips—License Plate and Twenty Questions. We also killed our share of enemy soldiers from the back window in a game where we shot imaginary Nazis traveling in other cars (tanks) on the road.

But beneath the games, the songs, and the family trips, my mother's unhappiness mounted. Tension showed in my parents' faces, but I have no stories of Mom throwing dishes in frustration, of Dad raising his voice in anger, or of either one furiously slamming doors. I knew when to steer clear of them, though: Mom raised one eyebrow when she was angry and her face darkened and grew stern. Dad's lips narrowed and he turned pale. I felt a chill in the air. With my parents' anger, one noticed more of a temperature change than a change in the decibel level of their voices.

Mom got frustrated and Dad would laugh it off or minimize her problem. To my childish mind it ended there, but for my mother, the hurts and slights accumulated. Neither of them aired their problems in front of the children, so we didn't realize the relationship was in trouble. My mother, the unhappy one, wanted more from the marriage and from her life. Nevertheless, I believe my father was content; his job offered him fulfillment where she didn't have that source of satisfaction. He failed to realize the depth of her distress, and she would say later he wasn't paying attention.

My mother channeled her emotions well, or else she denied them. She put her creative energy into redecorating and maintaining the house. I'd come home from school and see Mom, hammer in hand and a few nails clenched between her lips, going after something that needed repair. I'd walk in the door, put down my bookbag and lunchbox, often to find her under the sink fixing the plumbing or up on a ladder wallpapering. She was also a natural athlete. When she rearranged the furniture or worked in the yard, I could see the well-defined muscles in her petite body.

Mom wanted to be an artist before she married, but her mother talked her out of going to art school. She drew cartoon books, using family members and pets as characters, often illustrating amusing events that had taken place. Some provide a window on her growing frustration with my father. One cartoon shows me standing in front of my father as he sits in his chair reading the newspaper. I have a baseball bat in one hand and a glove in the other. As he holds the newspaper up in front of his face, I say, "And what do *you* do for fun?"

In 1953, when I was seven years old, my mother took me into the kitchen and told me that Jay and I were going to have a baby brother or sister. But she said I mustn't tell anyone. Too excited to heed that part, I immediately ran down the street to my best friend's house. We dashed out to her back yard and jumped on the swings as I spilled my joyful news. With the pull of each upward swing, feet pointed to the sky, I got more and more excited about becoming a big sister. But a few weeks later, my parents left the house suddenly late one night, and the next morning Dad told me Mom was still at the hospital. She had "lost" the baby. I was too young to know that Dad's euphemism, "lost," meant she had miscarried, and several days passed before I finally understood. We went to the hospital to pick her up and I saw her sitting in a wheelchair, looking so small and sad. I wondered if the baby had died because I'd disobeyed my mother when I told my friend. I watched my mother carefully for a few days after that, wondering when, or even if, I'd see her laugh again.

• • •

When Dad came home from work, he would often lie on the couch before dinner to rest. I would rub his forehead and smooth out the wrinkles. His skin was a little shiny and oily, but I liked making him feel better. To me, there was no one more handsome than my father, and the fact that we had certain features in common—the same nut brown eyes and a tooth that's crooked in the front—pleased me. When one of my elementary school friends told me her father was handsomer than mine because hers didn't wear glasses, I seethed for days.

Sunday afternoons in our family meant going for a drive for ice cream or root beer. Sometimes, the drive was interrupted by the wail of an ambulance siren or a fire engine. Jay and I cheered if our reporter father chose to follow the sound, hoping to capture the story of a blaze or accident for the next day's *Washington Star.* When at his desk, he always seemed to be talking on the phone about giraffes, but I realized later he was dictating stories and saying the word, "Paragraph."

My father prized self-sufficiency. If we were sick on a school day, we went anyway. Dad looked at things through the lens of a combat soldier, as if to say, "You're not bleeding, you're intact, so buck up." All of us—his children and his wife—felt the sting of his sarcasm. He made light of troubles you brought to him. We were not to complain. We were alive, after all, and many of his wartime buddies were not.

I was ten years old in the summer of 1957 when Dad left the *Washington Star* to go into business for himself and buy the *McLean Providence Journal,* a weekly newspaper in a town ten miles away. We moved there early that December. It was financially risky, because McLean, Virginia, was then a small, provincial town. But Dad knew there would be population growth, and he had the vision to be in the right place at the right time. He quickly learned the name of every volunteer firefighter, post office worker, and local shopkeeper. People praised my father's fairness and accuracy as a reporter, and if he wrote a half-inch more about one candidate in a race than another, his regular readers teased him for showing favoritism.

My mother's warm and lively manner brought her the affection of people in McLean. Had Dad been more sociable, they would have entertained and been part of the social scene. But he was content to stay home with the family and read. Books, newspapers, and his work were his oxygen, where other people and activity were hers. She was involved in school fund-raisers and community activities. She enjoyed writing a column for his newspaper but resented the fact that he never paid her for it.

During his tenure as editor and publisher of the *McLean Providence Journal,* McLean and the surrounding county of Fairfax grew rapidly. The nearby Tysons Corner area expanded from the tiny intersection of two country roads to the largest concentration of retail sales on the East Coast, second only to Manhattan. The Central Intelligence Agency came to town, and McLean became home to diplomats, members of Congress, high-ranking government officials, and entrepreneurs.

My father followed a journalistic code seldom seen today. Reluctant to invade the privacy of McLean's most famous people, he rarely covered their activities in the newspaper. Ethel Kennedy, who lived at Hickory Hill in McLean with her large family, expressed her appreciation of that policy. If Dad ran an item about the Kennedys, it was more likely to name the winners of the family pet show than the glittering dignitaries who attended their parties.

A real "shoe-leather" reporter, my father phoned the police dispatcher once an hour, looking for new stories since his last call. On one occasion, he even arrived at the scene of a bank robbery before the police. Jay told me once that Dad had given him some strange advice over the years; as an example, he cited how Dad cautioned him to always look through the window of a bank before entering. To Jay, this showed Dad's nervousness and hypervigilance, and that's probably so, but now that I've heard about his early arrival at the bank robbery scene, it's understandable—especially when one considers his war experience and aversion to loud noises, guns, and surprises.

Our typical suburban life was typical only on the surface. Trouble loomed as Jay's adolescent struggles emerged. My parents were stressed by moving and launching the new business. Then, in 1958, when I was almost twelve, my mother became pregnant again and gave birth to our brother, George. Meanwhile, Jay was growing more sullen and alienated by the day, and my parents had no idea how to reach him. I stood by, nervously watching everyone bicker.

George was born on September 9, 1958. I came home from school that day, excited about the new baby and hoping to see him. But he was very small and had to stay at the hospital a few days longer. The house was quiet. Dad sat in his yellow armchair and told me that Taffy, the sweet cocker spaniel we'd had for ten years, and Tiger, our cat, had eaten poisoned meat out behind the house and had both died. I never questioned the story until Jay told me years later that Dad had had them euthanized, and I felt a sickening lurch in my stomach as it dawned on me that it was true. Was he worried the pets would hurt the baby, who was already fragile? Had he heard stories of cats sitting on babies and smothering them? Did he think the animals would pass on germs to the baby (perhaps remembering his little brother Georgie and his strep infection), or would they add too much to an already overworked household? My parents' hands were certainly full, with one sullen and rebellious teenager (Jay), another in the making (me), and now a new baby. Looking back on this incident from my perspective as an adult, I see this as one of the times my father, in his keenness to protect the family, went too far.

Later that same night, Dad went back to the hospital, leaving Jay and me alone in the house. Jay, who was fifteen and not yet of legal age to drive, took Mom's car and left without a word as to where he was going. I waited as the night grew long, getting more and more nervous, wondering what my parents would say if they knew he was out with the car. Finally, I heard him drive up and slam on the brakes. I looked out in time to see him rushing into the field behind our house. About twenty minutes later, he suddenly emerged out of the darkness and ran inside, frightened and crying. "I wrecked Mom's car," he sobbed. I peeked into the driveway, dreading what I'd see. Barbed wire stuck out of the crumpled hood. He'd gone drag-racing with friends and smashed into something, but managed to drive the damaged car home.

Eventually, I went back to my room and sat on my bed, stunned, thinking about the day I'd had. I tallied the events of the last twenty-four hours: First, I'd finally become a big sister; second, Taffy and Tiger had died, supposedly poisoned; and third, my out-of-control brother had wrecked the car. In addition, my parents were at the hospital and I didn't know when they were coming back. I curled up under the covers and stared at the wall, feeling scared, bereaved, and happy all at the same time. Dad must have been upset when he saw the car, but I have no memory of it.

•   •   •

Thirteen months after George arrived, my sister Marty was born. I was embarrassed when a classmate asked, "Are your parents *done* now?" What were they doing, having all these babies? I didn't want to know. I'd wanted a new baby, but not necessarily one every year. Meanwhile, I tried to be the child my parents didn't have to worry about, so I could conceal my secret fear that Dad loved me less because I didn't have the sweet nature of my sister Marty, the irreplaceable charisma of his first-born son, Jay, or the pea-in-a-pod likeness to him of George. But mostly I felt invisible—unseen and unheard—lost in the crowd between my troubled and angry older brother and the demands made on my parents by my little brother and sister.

During my teens, my once happy rapport with Dad deteriorated, and we negotiated the changing relationship poorly. Especially painful were moments when I would attempt to snuggle with him in his big reading chair by the fireplace. I sometimes tickled him (always a disaster), and then he would bend my arm around behind my back or bend my fingers back until I fled the room, crying and baffled by what had become of my attempt to give and get affection. Dad retreated behind his newspaper or book, and Mom fumed at him in silence. The same scenario would be repeated years later between my father and sister.

I was a typical teenager in that I both hated and adored my family. I was even fiercely proud of Jay, whose brushes with the law were becoming more frequent and more serious. He was a talented poet, and I saw him as a misunderstood genius. I wanted to shout to my friends at school, "Can't you see how smart he is? And he has more soul than any of you." At the same time, my whole family mortified me and sent me into fits of rage. The only ones exempt from my resentment and embarrassment were the little ones, George and Marty. George was the image of our father, down to the tall, skinny build and the dimple in his chin. He was brainy and funny. Marty was sturdier and black-haired, like Mom, with almond-shaped dark eyes. Her eager-to-please personality and quick smile won everyone over. Yet we were growing up like two separate families, each consisting of two children, though under the same roof and with the same exhausted and frazzled parents.

Today, both my parents are gone, making me the sole custodian of our family history. I am the only one who was present in Jay's childhood and also in George and Marty's. I'm the bridge between the two, the link between both "generations." I would confound those who believe that birth order is destiny. For years I was the youngest, then at eleven I became the middle child. When Jay left home permanently when I was fourteen, I became the oldest, another mother to my younger brother and sister. As a result, I never really knew where I fit in.

My father's eccentricities embarrassed me. He didn't care about status and was almost anti-materialistic. I hunkered down in the seat of his beloved, ancient, and clunky car when he'd drop me off at school so no one would see me. At the same time, I admired his intellect and his integrity.

In high school, one of my friends said my father reminded him of Atticus Finch, the upright and moral lawyer who took on a racist town in *To Kill a Mockingbird*. When I told my mother, she nodded vigorously. "That's so true," she said. She shared his high principles but was sometimes annoyed when his unwavering code of ethics interfered with more practical matters.

For example, he refused to participate in Virginia's efforts to prevent school integration in the 1960s. During that time period, many Southern states, including Virginia, instituted a tuition grant system for parents of white children so that their children could attend private schools, the purpose being to avoid sending their children to the integrated public schools. The private school George and Marty attended *was* integrated and very progressive, and my father refused to take any of the money. He considered it dirty and found the idea of the state's actions to resist integration repugnant. My mother tried to convince him to be practical. After all, she reasoned, they both knew that wasn't why they were sending the kids to the private school, and they could use the money, so why not take advantage of the grant? But he wouldn't budge.

• • •

Dad's acute powers of observation resulted in an event that made an indelible impression on me when I was in high school. One afternoon as Dad mowed the lawn, he noticed a car parked under a tree on our street. It was unusual for anyone to park there, since the street was narrow and all the houses had long driveways. Mostly through instinct, he jotted down the license plate number and went back to his yard work. (He was never, even in relaxation, without a pen and paper.) Detectives appeared a short time later, fanning out to investigate an incident that had taken place in the neighborhood. When they saw Dad in the yard, they approached him, asking if he'd seen anything unusual over the course of the previous several hours. He told them about the car, then in his understated manner, pulled out his notepad, read off the plate number, and gave a description of the car, noting the exact time of day he'd seen it. The detectives were a little stunned by their luck. The suspect, later apprehended driving on the Capital Beltway, was subsequently convicted of raping a teenaged girl who lived up the street.

To my cousin Bill Dwyer, Dad personified manhood. He fondly recalled my father's five o'clock shadow and how scratchy it felt on his face when Dad bent down to greet him. Dad defined masculinity for me as well. I remember vividly the sound of his footsteps downstairs in the morning after he'd dressed for work. They were heavy, carrying the weight of authority and purpose, moving toward getting out the door and on with a productive day. Curled up in my bed upstairs, I felt safe. Even today, when I hear my husband walking downstairs with the same kind of shoes and the same kind of firmness, it brings back a feeling that all is right with the world.

But Dad saw hidden menaces in the world: germs, under-cooked food, dirty bathrooms and kitchens, contaminated water fountains, and strangers. Picking up money found on the street was forbidden to us. "You don't know where it's been," he'd say, as though anyone ever knew where money had been. He always ate meat well-done, for sanitary reasons. As a child, I never tasted meat that wasn't cooked to the consistency of leather. Once, in high school, I went to dinner at my friend's house and her mother made steak for dinner. "What was this? It was delicious! Why couldn't *my* family eat like that?"

In many ways he was as predictable as his food preferences. In other ways, his temperament was an unknown quantity. Things set him off that didn't seem so serious. When my friends toilet-papered our yard in high school (all the rage in 1963), he was so angry he turned red in the face and charged outside in his bathrobe and slippers, climbing up a tall pine tree to get the toilet paper down. My mother glared at me as we stood on the front porch watching him, and through gritted teeth, she said, "If he kills himself doing this, it'll be on you." I plunged my hands into my pockets and breathed in deeply as I kept one eye on my father, the other warily on my mother. I wanted to say, "It's only toilet paper!" But I warned my friends they'd better pass over our house next time.

The tension lurking behind the cool, Clark Kent exterior kept me on guard. I think of his war journal where he wrote, "Tight, tight, tight, and down, down, down." Dad was describing his desperate attempt to avoid being hit by incoming artillery, but he could have been describing his emotions.

After a leave in Paris, Ernie Pyle characterized what Dad and other combat soldiers would face when they returned to their former lives: "The gaiety and charm and big-cityness of Paris somehow had got a little on our nerves after so much of the opposite. I guess it indicates that all of us will have to make our return to normal life gradually and in small doses."[2] It was said of Pyle that after the war his "capacity for intimacy, never highly developed in the first place, was now severely strained."[3] Exactly the same could be said for Dad.

I could see that this quality—the lack of capacity for intimacy—as well as his rigidity frustrated my mother. One night he sat in his chair by the fireplace reading his newspaper. She stared at him for a long moment and said, "Why don't you grow a beard, or buy a Porsche, or do *something*?" He smiled a small smile and kept reading. It was as if he enjoyed being enigmatic and keeping her guessing.

Most of my efforts to get close to him, to hear him say "I love you," resulted in disappointment. The nearest I came was when he told me, in a rush of warmth as I left for college a few years later, "I think you're emerging from your awkward stage, dear." The backhanded compliment set my teeth on edge. At the same time, I was happy to receive any compliment from him. He often hid his emotions that way: A compliment would be camouflaged behind a mild putdown.

I went through college, graduating in 1969, then moved to faraway places that included Berkeley, Seattle, and Valencia, Spain. I missed my family during those years, 1969 to late 1971, but I needed to put distance between myself and the tension in our house. On my visits during this time, I noticed that my mother looked stressed and drawn and that the disquiet had begun to rise above the surface rather than roil beneath it. She snapped at Dad frequently and when he tried to take her hand, she pulled away. But after the visits I would go back to wherever I was living, and the letters I received from home were filled mostly with news of George and Marty's antics, so there was little to remind me of the lack of affection between my parents or to warn me of the impending catastrophe.

My mother left him about two months after their thirtieth wedding anniversary. It was winter, soon after Christmas in 1971, on a day that dawned as gray as gunmetal. I arrived for the holidays from Valencia, Spain, where I was living. I'd come home for what I thought would be a warm family get-together, my first in over a year and a half.

My father was at work on Wednesday, December 29, when my mother backed a truck up the driveway and removed half of the furniture. Jay nervously cracked jokes with Mom about "hazardous duty pay" when she asked him to help her. He and I reassured each other that the Luger in the basement was inoperative. But I couldn't bear the tension and anxiety, and that morning I left town for a few days. George and Marty were too young to take meaning from the undercurrent of tension that had been running through the house lately, although they surely sensed it.

Mom was afraid to alert Dad to her intentions in advance, for fear of what he might do—his years of over-controlled emotion might come raging forth through the broken dam. Awful as we felt about her actions, the "grown-up" children (Jay and I, at the time age 28 and 25, respectively) understood her reluctance to give Dad fair warning. She completed the move to her new home that day and returned to the house in McLean, picking up George and Marty on the way. Mom wanted to tell her husband that the marriage was over and that she'd moved out before he walked into the half-empty house and saw for himself. She was less nervous now, perhaps feeling protected by the younger children's presence or buoyed by finally having acted on something she'd wanted for so long. After she told him, he simply stood on the front lawn, his shoulders uncharacteristically sagging. She said later that he looked "shattered." The four of them—my parents, George, and Marty—stood, shifting nervously, in front of the house while the kids decided where they wanted to live. They chose up sides: Twelve-year-old Marty went on Mom's team, thirteen-year-old George on Dad's.

From that cold winter day onward, Dad and George began their "bachelor" life at our old family home where Dad's cooking skills centered around grilled cheese sandwiches. When I visited, I often heard the sad strains of "Bridge Over Troubled Water" or "I Can't Stop Loving You" on the stereo. Never really understanding why she left, he asked me repeatedly, "Do you know what your mother has in mind?"

A few days after Mom moved out, Dad asked me to meet him for coffee at McDonald's in McLean. I was getting ready to go back to beautiful Valencia, where I had a first-rate bilingual job, an apartment, a little Vespino motorbike, and a dark-eyed Spanish boyfriend. Dad was asking to see me not for the coffee but to beg me to stay home. I had never seen him plead for anything, and to say it broke my heart is an understatement. It made me feel sick. I had compassion for him but I seemed to have the backbone of a jellyfish—all I could think of in my hyperanxiety was how to escape this horrible situation. Mom had given me no hint of her plans to leave him, so her move came as a terrible shock. What had happened to them while I was living in Spain? The earth had shifted profoundly beneath me; the family I counted on had crumbled. At the same time, I felt guilty for not staying, for not fixing it, for not taking care of my father, and for thinking of myself. I couldn't put this right because it was too big for me. I was so afraid I would let him down. It was easily the worst day of my life.

"Please, honey," Dad said, "I need you here now." These words were so unfamiliar, the emotions so foreign. Need? I tried to remember "need" ever having been mentioned in our home—emotional need, at least. "I can't stay," I mumbled through a mouthful of guilt. Later that day, I left for New York, where I would board a plane for Valencia. I finally took off, exhausted but relieved to leave behind the mess that was now my family.

Back in Valencia, I tried to immerse myself in my Spanish life. Full of sadness and self-reproach, I began drinking too much. One night at 2 A.M., behind the wheel of my boyfriend's new sports car, not wearing a seatbelt, tipsy, and driving too fast, I ran a yellow light at an intersection and hit a Catholic priest whose car had started off too soon from the light. Thrown from the car, I nearly landed in the polluted River Turia. Somehow, the priest was unhurt, and he visited me each day in the hospital. Fifty stitches in my head and face, a dislocated shoulder, and a slight skull fracture kept me there for a week.

My life was unraveling and the earth beneath me grew even more unsteady as I felt my physical vulnerability after the accident. I was shaken to realize that my anchor, my family, was gone, or at least irrevocably changed. What, or whom, could I depend on now? Even when things at home were in an upheaval, I'd always known there *was* a home, and I'd believed my parents loved each other through it all. I never dreamed they would divorce.

I needed to go home, so I gave up my beautiful apartment, quit my job, and said adiós to my boyfriend. (I didn't need to sell the Vespino since it had been stolen while I was in the hospital.) I was on a plane bound for home barely a month after I had left my father at McDonald's, holding an empty cup.

•   •   •

Meanwhile, Dad took the box from Braunau and removed the phone bills and notes he'd kept there, replacing them with his

Army medals and the Bible his parents had given him as a boy. He clung to the box as a symbol of a time when his purpose on earth was more clearly defined: Fighting Nazi tyranny to protect the free world provided a clear goal for soldiers and citizens of the World War II era. Or perhaps my father was looking to replace the meaning my mother had taken with her when she left.

Only days after Mom left, Dad saw his nephew, Bill Dwyer, at a family gathering, and the two men talked about war. Bill had recently returned from a year's duty in Vietnam, where he served in combat with an infantry company and was awarded a Bronze Star. He knew my father had served in the Army many years earlier, but Vietnam was a very different war. The country was in a different mood—war protests were widespread, and U.S. efforts were winding down. Bill later recalled their meeting:

> I wasn't coming home with much pride in what I had accomplished or confidence in the war. Very few people wanted to talk about my time in combat, and those who did couldn't connect with me.
>
> It was [soon after] Christmas, 1971, I was in DC and saw Uncle Bill. I'd grown up with a special connection to him because we carried the same name. Now we had another tie: We'd both served our country under fire. But I'd always known Bill as a war hero who'd served in a just cause. I knew he wasn't in favor of the Vietnam War and I was unsure of how he would respond to me. At one point during a gathering of the family, he pulled me aside for a few private moments.
>
> He was kind, gentle, and let me talk. His own past experience created a safe bond. We were soldiers and family. In the thirty minutes of privacy, I talked and he listened with his heart and his eyes. I was able to pour out a lot of my heart, my frustrations, my sadness, and my anger over what I had seen,

and a few specific scenes that brought tears to my eyes. He just listened and I sensed he loved me, was proud of me, and understood me. The politics were not the issue. I was his nephew and he was helping me process. It was a very sweet moment. Although I never asked him, I always wondered: Was anyone there for *him* when he returned from Europe twenty-six years earlier?

NOTES

1. Ernie Pyle, *Brave Men* (New York: Henry Holt, 1944), p. 493.

2. Ibid., p. 490.

3. David Nichols, ed. *Ernie's War: The Best of Ernie Pyle's World War II Dispatches*, (New York: Touchstone/Simon & Schuster, 1986).

CHAPTER FIVE

"Elvin, Can You Take This Town?"

"Every platoon leader had to . . . realize that, if he made any
mistakes, men—flesh-and-blood human beings whom he
knew and may have befriended—could die."

—John C. McManus, *The Deadly Brotherhood*

The soldier closest to sustained and bloody combat during
World War II was the infantryman. Of the millions of American soldiers sent by the Army to foreign shores during the war,
only 14 percent were infantrymen, but that 14 percent ac-
counted for more than 70 percent of all battle casualties. Historian John C. McManus writes:

> There was no more perilous job [than the rifleman in an infantry
> division]. For the ground combat soldier, there was little doubt
> about what the future held. Eventually, if a man spent any
> significant time in combat, he would be killed or wounded. He
> could only hope that it would be the latter and not the former. If
> a man was wounded, he could hope to get out of combat for a
> time. If he was very lucky, he might get a so-called "million-
> dollar wound," an injury that was bad enough to keep him

permanently out of combat but not bad enough to cripple him for life.[1]

It was, as Dad told my brother Jay in the letter he'd written in case of his death, "a hazardous occupation."

There were other distressing (though less lethal) enemies faced by the infantrymen: food shortages, weather and terrain conditions, and trench foot. Trench foot, caused by prolonged exposure to dampness and cold, was the cause of terrible discomfort and sometimes resulted in gangrene and amputation. Infantrymen were given winter clothing and combat boots, but it was impossible to keep their feet dry in the mud and rain.

On September 27, 1944, the 318th was in Bratte, France. The month of September had been exhausting for the entire Division. Their race across France had been exhilarating at first, but the battle for the Moselle bridgehead had quickly turned into a grinding affair. The 318th Infantry, 2nd Battalion moved to Ville-au-Val for much needed rest and reorganization after being relieved by the 317th, 1st Battalion, but their rest lasted only a short while.

> *We slept in beds and ate hot meals. We ran night patrols from Landremont to Ste. Genevieve and back without incident. But about 10 days after we had come off Mount St. Jean, it became obvious that our rest was nearing its end. The word was that Patton had gone up to Landremont, looked far into the distance, and said, "General, I want those hills." And, so the story went, General Patton promised to send enough trucks to bring back the dog tags—identification carried by every GI and surrendered in death.*
>
> *But General Patton was popular. It was usual to hear a soldier say that if he ordered an attack, "You know you're goin', and everybody else is goin', too."*

When Patton looked into the distance from Landremont, the hills he said he wanted were Mount Toulon and Mount St. Jean, both overlooking the Seille River just east of the larger Moselle. German troops still held this high ground that divided the Moselle from the Seille, and Patton made it the focus of the next attack. Under cover of darkness, the Germans made nightly advances to the river to intercept any American patrols that might dare to attempt a crossing for reconnaissance purposes. The infantry was to take the small town of Manoncourt-sur-Seille and then prepare to cross the Seille itself.

> *OCTOBER 7, 1944, Manoncourt, France—Late in the afternoon we went up to the edge of the woods to go over the plan of attack. From our observation point, we could see the spire of the church in Manoncourt, our objective. The ground between us and the town was so level that it hurt to think about crossing it.*
>
> *The night was cold and foggy and we were all worried again. About three o'clock in the morning, the eerie stillness was broken by a heavy, hollow voice from the heavens, the Voice of Doom: "Soldiers of the 318th! We advise you to surrender. Come over to us and someday you will see your wife or sweetheart. Come with your mess kit in your hand and we will feed you. Do not delay, soldier. Tomorrow may be too late!" Our attack wasn't going to be a surprise.*

October 8, 1944, Manoncourt—The infantrymen awoke early that Sunday to gray skies and fog, unaware that this would be the 80th Division's "bloodiest day," when approximately 115 men would lose their lives. The full-fledged, coordinated onslaught to push the enemy back across the Seille was supported by a large body of fighter planes, three cannon companies, nine artillery battalions, tank destroyer guns, and one company of 4.2-inch chemical mortars.

At 0600 [6 A.M.], the first line moved out. Every man seemed to look to the right and left to be sure he wasn't alone, then a line of soldiers as far as the eye could see moved out into the foggy field.

We crossed several hundred yards without seeing friend or enemy. We found some heavy machine guns that were guarding the right flank of the attack. Things got stalled up front, there was firing. Our artillery was blasting away at the town. Across a line of trees to my right I saw a platoon approaching; must be F Company. As they came nearer we could hear them talking.

They weren't talking English.

I squirmed into firing position. Nobody fired but everyone was ready. We were face to face with struggle again.

Suddenly the two How [H] Company machine guns opened up. One of my mortar men dropped back and laid several rounds in the middle of the Jerries, not 50 yards in front of us. That was shooting!

I found the man in my platoon who could speak German. He shouted for them to surrender and we all took up the shout, but not one came in. The ones who were not hit by the machine guns, mortars, or our riflemen were captured later in the day.

Fox [F] Company was attacking Manoncourt itself. They had a number of casualties, especially at the Chateau where a German officer was directing the defense. My machine gun section went up on the hill beyond the town and got caught in a bad barrage. There were more prisoners than I had ever seen.

For the next several days, the two armies exchanged attacks and counterattacks, but ultimately the 80th strengthened its defenses in the Seille Valley. The Division had subdued the enemy and captured more than 1,260 German soldiers. The period after the October 8 attack until the end of the month was fairly static, with no further significant battles.

We had moved between Manoncourt and Clemery several times. The Krauts always seemed to know when the companies were exchanging positions; there were some casualties but a great deal more sweating it out.

Carr, Blanchard, and Pete Rigg all took out patrols. Carr had gone right up to a Jerry foxhole and dragged out a prisoner; he got the Silver Star for that. Blanchard was getting nervous as the works of a warped watch. Pete Rigg kept going out until one night he came back with holes in his shoulder and his cheek; a booby trap got him.

Nearly every night, patrols sneaked through treacherous enemy lines to bring back the exact location of German positions as well as data on the Seille River. The patrols were coordinated between the commanding officers and the S-2s, the regimental officers for military intelligence (the collection, evaluation, interpretation, and distribution of information about the enemy). No one was sure if the Germans were moving in additional defensive personnel, who were digging zigzag trenches to strengthen their defensive line and block any American attack, or if they were strengthening their forces, perhaps with tanks, for a counterattack. Additional enemy strength could signal to the U.S. commander that he should ask for more artillery and air support and indicate whether he should consider delaying his attack until he received sufficient fire support.

In the days leading up to November 7, the 80th held tight to its positions west of the Seille. Sweeping rains continued to flood the area, bringing the ubiquitous mud up to the soldiers' knees in places. A secondary purpose of the night patrols was to determine whether the Seille was fordable.

One day we were back at the Moselle practicing river crossings when the S-2 came up and told me the Major wanted me to take a combat patrol into Rouves that night. A jeep was waiting. The jeep driver waited for me near the cemetery while I sneaked out on the hill to look things over.

When I came back, I made a large sketch of the operation, then went down to the barn to orient the men. I knew we were in for a bad time; even a small enemy patrol could cause us plenty of trouble at the river.

Dad's nerves were on edge as he awaited orders to move out on patrol in the early evening hours of November 3. Thoughts spun through his mind as though he were dreaming.

Just before we got ready to move out there was a movie: Fred MacMurray and one of the Lane sisters in a musical. Reality and unreality swirled around in my brain; I was seeing a picture of a combat patrol and pretty soon we would go to a night club but what is the barn doing here? I was seeing a barn but Fred MacMurray was going out on patrol. I was dreaming of a barn, a dance band, and a patrol all at once. Soon it would be time to get up.

After the movie, I went back to the Company CP. I went through my belongings. The items that might be important I left in a box and told Carr where it was. I checked my carbine, had something to eat, and then sat down to wait. When the order came to move out, I shook hands with Capt. Chmar [who was now company commander]. *I could tell from his expression that I was not alone in expecting trouble. He said, "I know you'll do the job."*

Dad may have checked to make sure the letter he'd written to Jay was in the box. Perhaps he reread and pondered the words he'd written:

. . . I am not pessimistic, but, after all, being an officer in a rifle company comes under the heading of hazardous occupations . . . Do not grieve for me. I was fortunate above most men . . . in your mother's love and my love for her I found a fulfillment and a happiness such as few men could know if they lived a dozen lifetimes . . .

About six of the men carried the rubber boat as we moved out of Manoncourt. All day long I had known the waiting kind of fear, "sweating it out." As we moved down over the hill and across the flat field to the river, the action kind of fear came over me. It was the kind that makes the speech of men in combat a continual stutter. But you are busy while the action fear is on you and something inside you keeps saying, "Well, this is it and so far it isn't so bad."

We spread out along the river and the first squad started to cross. It was probably a fairly quiet affair, but to me it sounded like a combination bridge party and construction job. I left the sergeant to direct the rest of the crossing and eased into the next boat.

As the men crossed they moved to the right or to the left as we had planned—just as I had done in a similar exercise months before at Camp Croft. When the sergeant told me that everyone was across, I waved my arm forward, signaling the men to "move out." Two or three of us were on our way, but the whole line wasn't moving. I went all the way to the left, then to the right, then back to the middle. We were on our way into German territory.

The night was probably perfect for patrolling. We could see outlines 20 or 30 yards away, and on our right we could make out the line of trees that formed our right boundary. We had an incentive to speedy action: About 11 o'clock a full moon would be out.

We reached the first fence and some of us crossed it very cagily because of possible booby traps. But along came a couple of men who barged right into it and established that it wasn't charged. Then we reached the second fence, then the muddy road, now the shack.

Again I went back to make sure we would be at full strength when we hit the town. Other officers had taken out patrols and arrived at their objectives with half-a-dozen men. This wasn't going to be one of those.

We worked now with frantic speed. A few machine guns in the edge of town could have raised hell with us. We moved right up to the edge of town, some men up against buildings, others in gardens, others in alleyways. According to plan, I was to throw a grenade. When it exploded, every man was to fire his weapon or throw a grenade. I reached into my field jacket and pulled out the grenade. About 20 yards in front of me was some kind of weapons emplacement. I grasped the grenade firmly, pulled the pin, and heaved it. There was an explosion.

It was 10:30. The Jerry weapons opened up on us almost simultaneously, some from the left, some from the right. But none from the town itself. There was a noise in the building just to my left. I crawled over toward it and emptied my carbine into it. I realized that no one else was firing; I shouted for them to "cut loose" as I reloaded. I turned to try to bother one of the machine guns on our left. Our men were busy now. Rifles, automatic rifles, and grenades. Bullets were coming in close now, singing across the field.

I turned to the left again and fired at the brrrrrrp brrrrrp brrrrrrp and crrrrraaaak crrrrrrraaaak. Then a bigger gun to our left started throwing huge loaves of fire. My carbine was out of ammunition. I realized that the fire of the men had slowed down considerably. I gathered all my breath and shouted, "Let's go!" I took one last look at the enemy gun positions, trying to memorize them.

I could see the men running back toward the river. It seemed foolish to run through the gunfire but after the sergeant and I had crept and crawled a few yards, we realized we were going to be left. We got up and took off for the riverbank.

We were almost to the river when we got caught in a flare. Our objective was only 30 yards away so without a word, the sergeant and I made the same decision: a few steps and one last great leap and we were under cover on the riverbank. The firing was heavy now. A new gun down the river to the right had joined in.

The first boatload crossed and took off for greener pastures. On the second trip, the rope used to pull the boat broke. One of the men tried to paddle it back, but it was an almost hopeless task for one man. I told two men in the next group to come back with the boat; only one of them did. The boat spun crazily around in the middle of the stream. Mortars began to fall downstream from us.

Several men couldn't wait for the boat. As they attempted to swim the river to safety—loaded down with ammunition, weapons, and heavy clothing—they frantically clawed at the water and were pulled beneath the swirling river. The brother of one of the men who died came to see Dad years later to learn about his brother's last moments. Dad told me he gave him an account of what had happened, but wished he hadn't. "It didn't make him feel any better," Dad said, his eyes downcast and his mouth pulled tight in a grim line at the memory.

There were men trying to get to the other bank without help from the boat. There was the sound of splashing near the other bank, two horrible drowning sounds, and then no more. The next mortar barrage was closer. The boat was loose again. I reached out and grabbed it and told the next group of men to hurry. A soldier tapped me on the shoulder. There was someone coming down the hill from Rouves. I pulled my carbine into firing position, but as the figure drew closer I recognized one of our own men.

The boat was on its way back again. We waited and waited and waited. Every last man got in. As we trudged up the hill carrying the boat toward our own lines, a mortar barrage landed right on our crossing point. As we reached our own lines, the Germans dropped some more about 100 yards from the river. They were on our trail, but too late.

Dad had carried one of his wounded men down to the boat and was the last man to leave the shore for the safety of the opposite bank. They hoisted the wounded into the last boat and hurriedly pushed off for the friendlier side of the river. By way of greeting they received a shot from their own lines.

When they reentered Rouves five days later on November 8, Dad realized there were many more Germans there than they'd previously thought. The Germans had been sleeping and were caught off guard when Dad's patrol arrived. Dad doubted that many of his men would have returned alive had the Germans been waiting for them on top of that hill. "It was a foolish, foolish patrol," he said later. "But it was standard procedure—they'd send out a patrol to see what was out there."

My father was awarded the Silver Star for gallantry in action for leading this patrol. Silver Stars were not passed out often during World War II. In fact, in the 80th Division, only 671 men were awarded Silver Stars. Dad's citation says:

> While returning from reconnaissance patrol deep in hostile territory on November 3, 1944, Lt. Elvin and his comrades received heavy machine gun fire. With disregard for personal safety, he advanced alone through the heavy concentrations, destroyed the positions, and returned to his patrol carrying a casualty. He then led his men to safety. Lt. Elvin's courage and outstanding leadership exemplify the highest traditions of the armed forces of the United States.
>
> *Two men had drowned; one man had been wounded in the arm. The rest, except for being wet, were OK.*

The major had promised Dad a bottle of Scotch and a trip to Paris, but all promises were forgotten the next day as preparations got under way for a new and all-out attack.

During the previous month of October, twice the amount of rain fell as during a normal year. Every day and every night it poured; the streets, fields, and streams saw the worst flooding in the history of the area. The Seille River rose to several times its normal width and spewed over its banks. Despite this month-long deluge, General Patton had designated the morning of November 8 for the next major assault. The day before the planned attack, sheets of rain fell for twenty-four hours straight, but Patton could hold off no longer and delivered the code words "Play ball."

The streets of Clemery, the jumping-off point for the strike, were underwater as the 80th Division launched early that morning. They attacked with three regiments abreast, the 318th in the center. The 2nd Battalion of the 318th would later be cited by Major General McBride for its extraordinary heroism, gallantry, determination, and esprit de corps in overcoming hazardous and difficult conditions against the enemy that day.

Company E would cross first after a great artillery barrage. We were to move up the hill and take care of the guns that had fired on the patrol, then swing down into Rouves. By 0500 [5 A.M.] on the morning of November 8, our artillery was already booming. The show was on, flood or no flood.

We moved to the riverbank and waited for the order to cross. It was still dark when the engineers pulled our boats to the other side. We reorganized and moved away from the river. Chmar, Blanchard, Carr, and myself got lined up for the push; we moved straight up the hill as flocks of mortars landed on the river crossing.

Our men were firing as they advanced; it was risky moving from side to side as we moved up. At the top of the hill we swung to the right to go down into Rouves.

We kept firing. A Kraut machine gun was firing toward us but we couldn't hear the bullets. The sergeant who had been in charge of my machine gun section on Mount St. Jean was killed by a bullet that hit him in the head.

One of his friends ran over to see what was the matter with him. Then the friend, stony-faced, told us, "That guy's dead," and we moved on.

Now Rouves was in sight. Just as we were moving into the building there was shouting: "Hold your fire!" That meant prisoners. I looked down the main street; white flags and handkerchiefs were fluttering in the doorways. We came into the street and told the prisoners to come out. The first group numbered about a dozen.

We were low on ammunition but Chmar decided to try to push on through town. He was as imperturbable as he had been when he moved among the men on Mount St. Jean, a blanket over his shoulders.

I saw a Kraut far down in the town square. I shouted to him to "come here." He stopped and turned around, ran to the edge of a building, and sprayed the street with machine gun fire. The platoon guide of the second platoon moved down the street to the left and got hit about 20 feet in front of us. Then a grenade exploded at his feet. He lay very still.

Chmar decided to take the same route; I tried to discourage him but he went along the same wall. A bullet whipped through the back of his leg. He laughed and came limping back; as he passed the same point again he got clipped again in the leg.

Captain Chmar had been wounded earlier near the Moselle. He had the shrapnel removed from his leg and then he insisted he be returned to lead his company. After the second wounding in Rouves, he was evacuated to an English hospital.

When the platoon guide was hit I thought the fire had come from a hole in the wall at his feet, but now I was sure that the weapon was on the other side of the street. I called the bazooka-man. He stood in the middle of the street with his bazooka pointing toward an open second-story window that seemed to be the immediate objective. I got the men out from behind the bazooka and directed small arms fire on the window while the bazooka-man aimed.

The shot was good; it was hard to believe that there could be anything left alive in that room. But now we were almost out of ammunition and would have to wait for a re-supply.

Major Gardner came up and asked for the situation. Chmar told him what had happened. The Major asked me if I thought I could go through the town; I told him I thought I could.

"When the company commander [Chmar] got hit," Dad said, "the major said to me, 'Elvin, can you take this town?' What could I say? I said, 'Yes, sir.' "

We were just entering the square when we caught a volley of small arms fire. Three men were killed; the rest of us scattered. I was behind a wall on the left side of the square. Some of the men were firing at the enemy riflemen and machine gunners in the stone church but the Krauts were shooting out of narrow slits and we were almost in the open.

I looked around for the bazooka-man; I couldn't see him so I shouted for him. We were stopped cold; our only chance was to get a few good bazooka rounds into that church.

I took a firm grip on my carbine and dashed across the street. I found the bazooka-man and showed him where I wanted him to fire. Only one man could fire from that side of the street without getting into the open. It would be impossible for me to direct the fire without getting back on the other side of the street; from there I could see the church and my men on both sides.

I grasped my carbine again and scooted across the street; just as I was saying to myself, "You made it," I had a strange feeling that I was hit somewhere. I got down behind the wall. There was blood on my left hand. I wondered what had happened to my stomach; there were holes through my two field jackets.

One of the men was standing up and firing back at Krauts. He asked, "Get hit, Lootenant?"

The bazooka-man was calling; his round had landed about two feet away from one of the slits, [but] had done no appreciable damage. I told him to fire again; no more ammunition.

We were getting nowhere and from the position we were in, we never would. I never thought so much of our men as I did while they stuck their heads above the wall and fired at Germans who were almost fully protected.

I told them to stay under cover; I would go back to see the Major. I started to go back but I just couldn't. The same sharpshooter would be looking for me again.

But everything had stopped and I was bleeding and something had to be done. I picked up my carbine and took off. I raced through a building, a barn, and some houses. Several of our men were huddled in between the buildings. Across the street was the building where I had left the Major; I ran across.

I told him we were stopped and would have to go around to the right. He told me that the medic was in a nearby shed; the wound in my arm looked much larger than it felt. The medic went through his routine: morphine, sulfa powder, sulfa pills, dressing, sling.

• • •

Several years ago, I saw an item in the *Blue Ridge*, the 80th Division newsletter, that sent chills down my spine. It was an inquiry from a man whose grandfather had been killed by a sharpshooter in Rouves on November 8, 1944—probably the same sharpshooter who had wounded my father at 8 A.M. that same day. The *After Action Report* for that day said that at 9:15 A.M., the sniper was still shooting from the church tower. The sheer randomness of death struck me hard. It was so odd that because of the sniper, the man writing the letter had never known his grandfather, and given an inch or two of difference in a bullet wound, I might never have been born.

Dad had seen the bravery his men had shown. They'd risked their lives to cover him in battle. The relationship of officers to their men put the officers in a unique position. As historian John C. McManus writes:

> At the same time that they shared and experienced the awful realities of war with their men, junior officers [platoon leaders, company commanders, and so forth] were also directly responsible for the welfare of those men. Every platoon leader had to live with the knowledge that his chances of becoming a casualty were even greater than the chances of those he commanded. In addition, he had to realize that, if he made any mistakes, men—flesh-and-blood human beings whom he knew and may have befriended—could die.[3]

Lieutenant Walter Carr noted that the men sometimes saw officers as the enemy, the ones who made them do all the things that would get them killed. "But it's the president of the United States who's giving the orders that are being carried out all along the line," said Carr. "If you're the officer down there, you're carrying out what the Commander-in-Chief tells you."

Of course, there was the occasional officer who was not beloved and deserved little or no respect. In conversations with veterans at reunions of the 80th Division, I've heard several stories about the "lowly" enlisted man who confronted a "ninety-day wonder"—the enlisted man's name for an officer who'd received his ninety days of training but was shy of combat experience—for his ignorance, ineptitude, or even cowardice. Usually, it was the case that the officer's ninety days of training had given him an inflated sense of his own value or judgment, which brought resentment from the enlisted men. After all, it was the enlisted men who were carrying the brunt of the terrible work of war, and yet they were at the mercy, in a very real way, of their officers' leadership ability.

Good officers tended to lead their men rather than ensure their own safety. Walter told me that Dad didn't use his rank to avoid danger or ask his men to do anything he wouldn't do. Officers like Walter, Captain Chmar, Lieutenant Blanchard, my father, and many others were hard to replace. Morale could suffer when they were wounded and evacuated or killed. Ernie Pyle, in a well-known dispatch, "The Death of Captain Waskow," reported seeing a unit lose a beloved officer who had served with the unit since it left the States. The men carried his body from the front, and Pyle looked on as they said their last goodbyes.

> One soldier came and looked down, and he said out loud, "God damn it." That's all he said, and then he walked away. Another one came. He said, "God damn it to hell anyway." He looked down for a last few moments, and then he turned and left. Another man came; I think he was an officer. It was hard to tell officers from men in the half light, for all were bearded and grimy dirty. The man looked down into the dead captain's face, and then he spoke directly to him, as though he were alive. He said, "I'm sorry, old man." Then a soldier came and stood beside the officer, and bent over, and he too spoke to his dead captain, not in a whisper but awfully tenderly, and he said: "I sure am sorry, sir." Then the first man squatted down, and . . . took the dead hand, and he sat there for a full five minutes,

holding the dead hand in his own and looking intently into the dead face, and he never uttered a sound all the time he sat there. And finally he put the hand down, and then reached up and straightened the captain's shirt collar, and then sort of rearranged the tattered edges of his uniform around the wound. And then he got up and walked away down the road in the moonlight, all alone.[4]

More soldiers came up to replace the dead and the wounded. The door continued to revolve in the vicious cycle of war. My father was fortunate that his exit was—as Major Baresi had told them on that "forlorn hillside in Wales" back in July, when he'd welcomed them to the European Theater of Operations—on a stretcher and not in a coffin.

> *With two other casualties, I began the march back to the Seille with the prisoners. In Clemery, as I headed for the aid station and a drink of cognac, there were hundreds and hundreds of GIs waiting to press the attack.*

Sometimes Dad reflected on the war and the fatalistic thoughts he had while in combat. He later recalled:

> Perhaps you could take cover from small arms fire behind a rise, but you knew mortar fire and artillery could still get you. Other times you advanced across a field—open like a football field, and if you got through that it was sheer luck. You had no way to protect yourself. I'd think, just keep down and keep moving. If you got to a river—an enemy soldier with a machine gun and lots of ammunition could control the crossing and do terrible damage to our company.

There was no rotation system or tour of duty in this brutal and destructive war, only a revolving door: Do your duty to your country and your comrades and fight, be killed or wounded, and be replaced.

"The infantry just kept going," Dad said. "You lost people, others came up. That's how it was. The infantry just kept on going."

NOTES

1. John C. McManus, *The Deadly Brotherhood: The American Combat Soldier in World War II* (Novato, Calif.: Presidio Press, 2000), p. 132.

2. A.Z. Adkins, Jr., and Andrew Z. Adkins III,. *You Can't Get Much Closer Than This: Combat with Company H, 317th Infantry Regiment, 80th Division* (Havertown, Penn.: Casemate Publishing, 2005), p. 224.

3. McManus, op. cit., p. 202.

4. http://journalism.indiana.edu/resources/erniepyle/wartime-columns/.

CHAPTER SIX

A Door Closes and Another Door Opens

"A mere rustling curtain can paralyze a man with memories."
—Ernie Pyle, *Here Is Your War*

My parents had stopped communicating long before my mother decided to leave in 1971, but Dad hadn't seemed to notice. He always couched his rare expressions of emotion in vague language. Mom strained to decipher what he was thinking, but eventually her efforts turned to resignation and, finally, to resentment. When her unhappiness began to give her stomach problems and headaches, she made her decision to leave. Writing her own set of rules for a change, my mother set off to live a new life.

The summer after she left, 1972, was the first year in which no marigolds, zinnias, or snapdragons showed their colorful faces in the garden of our home in McLean. Without Mom to replant the garden, only the perennials returned—the hollyhocks, foxgloves, and gladiolas—but eventually even they succumbed to neglect. Still, the intoxicating and heavy fragrance of lilac floated once again through the kitchen window from the bush she had planted behind the house, a sensory reminder of her.

A few days after she'd moved out, my father had sat down with my brother George, who was thirteen and with whom Dad was now living. Dad said, "I imagine there are going to be times you feel like crying." George could just hear Dad thinking, "and I sure hope now isn't one of them."

"That was about the extent of our talk about the divorce," George later said.

•   •   •

The days acquired a rhythm for Dad and George: a morning walk with the dogs, Snoopy and Schweppes; breakfast before school at the Key Bridge Marriott. Dad packed George's lunch for school, usually two pieces of toast with butter and bacon, wrapped in Saran Wrap. Each weekend, George visited Mom. Meanwhile, my sister Marty lived with Mom and met Dad for a meal a few times a week.

The pallor in the garden matched the worn-out look of the house. Mice scampered inside from the fields and woods out back, and Dad set "Havahart" mousetraps that captured them without killing them. Then he'd take them out into the field and release them to the wild. The mice waited a few days before they ran back into the house.

The box from Braunau sat atop the dresser in Dad's bedroom. The box reminded him of the prisoners who'd been freed, of the people who'd been oppressed under the Nazi regime, and of the necessary will and might required to beat back the forces of repression and tyranny.

He was still unable to give a voice to the memories that haunted his mind and his dreams. A part of my father always remained detached, apart, and guarded. In those days, however, there was no official psychiatric name for what he was experiencing. Though the term Post-traumatic Stress Disorder

(PTSD) was first introduced in 1980 by the American Psychiatric Association in the *Diagnostic and Statistical Manual of Mental Disorders (DSM-III)*, no completely accurate description or understanding of this cluster of symptoms and how to treat them was available until the publication of the *DSM IV* in 1994. PTSD was defined as an anxiety disorder marked by the dissociation required to endure trauma—exposure to combat being one of its strongest triggers.

•   •   •

Over breakfast at our favorite deli in the summer of 2008, my friend Katie and I spoke to a World War II veteran who'd ambled by our table. He was wearing a cap with his Army division on it and I asked him where he'd served. Afterward, I told Katie that I had some discomfort labeling my father with PTSD because I knew that among some veterans it brings a dark cloud of shame. Katie, a trauma therapist, explained that PTSD is not a mental illness but a maladaptive reaction to a traumatic event. In other words, the constant and heightened alertness required for combat survival can cause overwrought anxiety if applied back home.

Serving as an officer may bring special anxieties. According to Lieutenant General John Vines, who led the 18th Airborne Corps in Iraq and Afghanistan:

> All of us who were in command of soldiers killed or wounded in combat have emotional scars from it. No one I know has sought out care from mental health specialists, and part of that is a lack of confidence that the system would recognize it as "normal" in a time of war.[1]

As Katie explained it to me, PTSD manifests itself in recurrent nightmares, difficulty with intimate relationships, trouble sleeping, extreme jumpiness (heightened startle reflex), disso-ciation and wariness, difficulty concentrating, and flashbacks. The person experiencing a flashback feels as though he or she has left his/her body and environment, often without any warning. After the first flashback, the person then feels ex-tremely wary of certain triggers, whether they are situations or people. To make matters worse, the individual may not know what those triggers are, resulting in even more guard-edness and hypervigilance.

PTSD can make a person more irritable and frustrated and can make a parent seem hostile or distant. Children of someone with PTSD symptoms might easily question the parent's love for them and misunderstand the reasons behind the symptoms. Research shows that children of veterans with PTSD are at higher risk for behavioral, academic, and interpersonal problems.

While it varied in intensity from child to child, in our fam-ily the continuing legacy of our father's wartime trauma was ap-parent in our lives. Dad, like many in the armed forces, fought bravely under extraordinarily brutal conditions, and then came home to live an ordinary life while at the same time justifying (to himself) having survived. The war never really ended for this man who'd always tried hard to do what was expected of him.

Ernie Pyle described in a dispatch what it might be like for the combat soldier to return to civilian life:

> It will be odd to drive down an unknown road without that little knot of fear in your stomach; odd not to listen with animal-like alertness for the meaning of every distant sound; odd to have your spirit released from the perpetual weight that is compounded of fear and death and dirt and noise and anguish . . . Our feelings have been wrung and drained; they cringe from the effort of coming alive again.[2]

• • •

Trips to the mountains offered my father solace and soothing refuge in the years following my mother's abrupt departure. He'd get in his car, the backseat filled with newspapers, the front seat with eight-track tapes of Frank Sinatra, Elvis Presley singing gospel, Barbra Streisand, and the Irish singer Frank Patterson. He'd set off northwest toward the Blue Ridge Mountains. He would steer the Impala over mountains called Bear, Shaffernaker, and Savage, eventually stopping in his childhood home of Frostburg, where he'd spent happy years. Frostburg changed little from year to year, and the view from the family burial plot atop the rolling hills of the cemetery still offered tranquility and reassurance. Dad's thoughts would circle back to his youth and to the happiness and security that had enveloped him. After driving by the houses his family had lived in and eating lunch at the Princess Restaurant, he would turn the car around and head back down into the lower and flatter ground of northern Virginia, returning refreshed and reconnected with his solid roots.

Those were lonely days for Dad, and I noticed that the bottle of Scotch in the corner cupboard was being drunk at a much faster rate than before. Meanwhile, my own lifestyle was nothing to be admired as I moved back and forth between my parents' homes, paying rent to neither one, and feeling hopeless about my future. I'd never been so unmoored as I was during those years. I scraped together the money for a car, but I ruined the engine within a few months, not knowing you had to keep an eye on the oil level. Waitressing gave me some cash, but not enough money to save. I tried to spruce up Dad's sad house by repainting the porch floor. One day I came home and it had peeled; I was unaware that floors required special paint.

My father needed looking after, I thought, because he was confused and unhappy. So was I. The only member of the family who seemed happy was Mom; all of a sudden, she was seeing to her own well-being instead of serving everyone else's needs. I was a bit taken aback by her new attitude. "What do you mean, you need your car tonight?" I'd say if she'd refuse my request to borrow her car. "*I* need your car."

During the times I lived at Dad's, I'd sometimes call him late at night for a ride home from the restaurant where I worked. Clad in his pajamas, bathrobe, and slippers, he'd often show up with liquor on his breath. Frightened by this unfamiliar father who slurred his words, I would go back and stay at Mom's for a while. Yet to all outward appearances, he was the same person. He strode around town attending to his newspaper business, and no one knew how much he suffered.

The things he cared about—such as family, the newspaper, his community, his reputation, books, poetry, politics, baseball, duty, his country, and world peace—didn't change. He was a charming man with an affable, cool exterior, but he had depth, as shown by his taste in poetry, which ran to the sensual and rich: Rudyard Kipling, W. B. Yeats, A. E. Housman, even Rumi, the Persian writer of love poems.

Dad was fascinated by politics—world and national, but especially local. One of the biggest moments in McLean history was the clash between its citizens and their county government in the mid-1960s. It involved the battle to forestall construction of a high-rise apartment building at Merrywood, the estate that was Jacqueline Kennedy's childhood home on the banks of the Potomac River. Citizens of McLean thought the apartments would be destructive of the river's shoreline beauty. My father deserves some of the credit, many in McLean believe, for preventing that construction, not through editorializing, but through honest reporting of the views of the whole community.

Politicians, their positions, and their occasional antics sometimes amused him. A Virginia congressman once called a news conference to announce that he was not, as had been alleged, the "dumbest" member of Congress. The fact that he'd called such a news conference delighted Dad, who phoned me and told me about it with a wry chuckle.

I'm sure he was privy to many secrets about the citizens of McLean, since as editor of the local newspaper he had access to police reports and other confidential information. Plus, he often used a reporter's trick to get people to spill secrets, one that plays into a person's need to feel important, or right, or "in the know." Acting like he knew much less than he did, he would play innocent and ask questions, and soon enough the person was telling all.

But within our family many topics were off limits and never spoken about: his brother Georgie, the camps he saw during the war, the divorce, his subsequent loneliness, money, and relationships. An undercurrent of tension and silence made me anxious, and I wondered uneasily if there existed a terrible secret I didn't know, and didn't want to know.

Complicit in the silence was the fact that never in 10 million years would I have sat my father down for a heart-to-heart talk because I didn't want to hear what he might say. Was the underlying hurt I'd sensed in him my fault? Or would hearing about it upset the fragile equilibrium we'd achieved in our relationship? I imagine many children of combat veterans have experienced the same feeling. As author Scott Turow said in an interview about his father, a veteran of World War II, we have a sense that "something had *happened* to Dad in the war."[3] While I felt the grip of sadness as I surveyed his lonely life, even stronger was my feeling of anxiety, its roots unknown at the time.

Within a year or two after Mom left, Dad began seeing a woman who managed his office, Elizabeth ("Lib") Raleigh, whom he'd known for years. Her wonderful deep-dimpled smile made you believe the world was a safe place. She brought a sense of normalcy and goodness into the family.

They'd make a day of an excursion to Frostburg. Going "over the horizon," he called it, and he discovered he liked to just take off and see what happened. This was quite a change from the controlled man who preferred to know what was coming down the "unknown road" to which Ernie Pyle referred. Gradually, their relationship morphed into a deep friendship that lasted for twenty-five more years until Lib passed away. She was an anchor in troubled times for all of us.

In 1992, Dad finally moved out of the dilapidated house, selling it for not much more than the value of the acre of land. The new owner made a verbal promise that he wouldn't raze the house and replace it with a "mega-mansion," as had happened with many houses on our street. But one day, I drove by and saw that our house was being used as the construction shack while a new and much larger house was built in front, occupying the entire front lawn. Quite a few years passed before Dad could bring himself to go back to see what had replaced our house.

He also began to lose hope that Mom would fall back into his arms. "It's been nearly ten years now," he said in 1980. "I don't suppose your mother's coming back." But moving out of the house signaled his acceptance that she was gone for good, and the change to an apartment was beneficial. The apartment was a cozy place, its sliding doors looking out onto a lovely view of a courtyard filled with fruit trees. Dates and weekly lunches with friends began to appear on his calendar along with business appointments. I noticed when I hugged my father now that it was no longer like hugging a telephone pole. More often he would actually hug in return, or at least not stiffen up. He even wrote sweet, funny notes on cards he sent to his children and grandchildren.

Nonetheless, he still had "quirks" and trouble connecting with people. The most evident, and to me, the most annoying, was his disconcerting habit of changing the subject of a conversation in midstream. He'd veer off without any warning or explanation, particularly if the topic strayed to the personal. Here's an example:

Jan: "I'm not sure if I should stay in this job any longer, if it's really for me."
Dad: "Oh?"
Jan: "I'm thinking of talking to a counselor about it."
Dad: "Well, I ran into Chuck and Lynda Robb the other night at a Democratic fund-raiser. They seemed to be in good shape."

The conversation illustrates two of the more common PTSD symptoms he displayed: avoidance and the need to be in control.

My father habitually told his children and even grandchildren what they did or did not need. Molly, Marty's daughter, had him pegged from a young age. One day when she was four, Molly ran into the apartment to see him, dark ponytail flying behind her. As she started back out the door for the playground, she popped her pacifier into her mouth. Dad stopped in the middle of putting on his coat, reached for the pacifier, and said, "You don't need that." She quickly removed it, but with one hand firmly grasping the pacifier and the other on her hip, she looked up at him and said, "I want it, I need it, and I'm gonna *have* it!" When my sister told me the story, I thought, "There's a new generation of Elvin women, and they're not going to put up with it like we did." Molly knew what she needed and wasn't afraid to tell him so, which I'd never had the nerve to do.

My own life had finally begun to make some sense as well. I went to work for the American Civil Liberties Union in

Washington, and at last I was able to translate my idealism into something concrete. I had previously worked for Ralph Nader, but that left me unsatisfied because the office was so disorganized and crazy. Dad approved of my involvement with the ACLU. In a card, he wrote, "Jan, what you are doing with your life brings joy and comfort to your old father." For the first time, to my eyes, he'd crossed over to my side and become proud of me. He saw me, at least professionally, if not personally.

My father's profound concern for justice once came out in a strange way. One day in late 1981, we met for lunch because I wanted to tell him I was planning to get married. He knew that Al Bronstein, my new love (and Anthony Quinn look-alike), had devoted his life to civil rights. A lawyer in Mississippi during the civil rights struggles of the 1960s, Al was now the leading force in the country for the rights of prisoners. Even though I was thirty-five, I had never really contemplated marriage before, but this relationship was deeper and more loving than anything I had known, and I was excited to share my news. Dad nodded when I told him our plans and said, "I always taught you to believe in civil rights."

My mouth dropped open and I couldn't think of anything to say. Of course, one basis for loving Al was his commitment to those ideals, but how odd, I thought, to hear Dad put that forth as the reason I was marrying him.

•   •   •

Despite an active and otherwise healthy lifestyle, nearly sixty years of smoking had ruined my mother's health. In 1997, she faced serious cardiac surgery. The night before her operation, I told Mom her surgeon had a great reputation, and then, as an aside, that he was a Mormon. "Good!" she said. "At least I know he won't be hung over."

My mother bled easily because of the Prednisone she took for her rheumatoid arthritis, and during the long heart surgery and subsequent days in the Cardiac Intensive Care Unit, she received more than twenty-one units of blood even though she only weighed 110 pounds. During the long night of one of her surgeries (she had three), nurses played a cassette tape of her granddaughter Molly singing, which the surgeons and nurses said calmed her down.

Thanks to the operations, she lived to go to the beach with all of us again and to celebrate her seventy-ninth birthday at a party she dubbed "a dress rehearsal" for her funeral. We sang the hymns her father used to sing on the porch in Cumberland and showered her with gifts and love. But by January 1998, her breathing problems grew worse. A few days after she was hospitalized again, we learned she had cancer that had metastasized to the lining of her lungs. Nothing could be done. I was in her room talking to a nurse about managing her pain when she passed away the evening of February 25.

The nurse threw a startled look toward Mom, and the air in the room flattened. It was as though the "fizz" had gone out of it. I looked aghast at the nurse, unable to believe that my mother was gone. She murmured that she'd never seen anyone die before as she lowered the bed so Mom would lie prone when rigor mortis set in. She asked me kindly what I needed her to do to help me now, and she told me to take all the time I wanted with Mom. Though I heard her words, I didn't understand her. I pulled my chair up close to the bed and scoured Mom's face for signs of life. My mother, so small and so dear to me, lay still while I waited for her to take a breath. I shook my head hard to bring back the effervescence around her, but it didn't work.

After a while I made the phone calls I needed to make, arranged for the funeral home to come for her body, and went out into the blackness of the cold February night for the drive home.

Ironically, earlier that week, both my parents had gone into the hospital at the same time. As my mother struggled for her last breaths at one hospital in Virginia, just fifteen miles to the east, a cardiac surgeon stopped my father's heart to perform a triple by-pass. A few more days in the hospital and Dad would leave for a stay at a rehab facility to recuperate.

During his hospital stay, I met Ruth McGoff, the director of Case Management at the Virginia Hospital Center in Arlington. Despite my fog (I was still reeling from racing back and forth on the Capital Beltway between the two hospitals), I noticed she was almost always at his bedside. One day after I visited him, Ruth walked me down the hall. She looked at me intently, and in her thick Boston accent, said, "Your *fathah* is an *extrahdinary* man."

Both my mother and father spent that week fighting for their lives, and at its end, she died and he lived. After I returned home the night she died, I phoned him to tell him the awful news. He reacted with shock, almost horror. I cringed as he let forth with a low moan, "Oh, no, oh, Lord, no!"

His long wait for her return was over.

Before Dad left the hospital, his doctors diagnosed him with pulmonary fibrosis, a progressive lung disease. But his heart was healing, in more ways than one. I believe my mother's passing freed him to begin a life-changing relationship. Now he could open up to love with a woman who was real and present in his life.

Late one afternoon in the early fall of 1998, Marty called me from Dad's apartment. She lowered her voice as she whispered into the phone, "I think he has a girlfriend—the woman from the hospital." Reaching back into my memory of those foggy and worry-filled days, I remembered Ruth. This was interesting news.

Later, I learned that they started having lunch together at the hospital soon after he joined the post-op cardio-rehab program. Every Thursday after his workout, they met in the cafeteria. About 50 percent of the time was spent talking about World War II; he shared his theories with her about how it could have been avoided. It surprised her to hear he'd fought in the infantry because he sounded like a pacifist, more of a global thinker and an internationalist than a nationalist. While he loved his country deeply and treasured its ideals, he didn't subscribe to the view of "America, right or wrong."

History seminars aside, he fell hard for Ruth and she for him. Ruth was considerably younger, rosy-cheeked and pretty in a comfy way, respected for her work, and politically attuned with Dad. They began to call each other "lad" and "lassie." She'd smile up at him and then, looking over at whoever else was there, say, "Isn't he a handsome lad?"

In fact, she made sure he looked good, which was a relief to me. When he'd gone into the hospital earlier that year, Marty and I went to get clothes from his house. We were embarrassed and shocked by the frayed collars, missing buttons, and worn-through pants. He didn't have one really decent outfit. But we didn't think we should be telling him what to wear, and we delighted in turning the matter over to Ruth. He *was* a handsome lad, especially in his new clothes, even at eighty years old—still tall and lean, with only a smattering of gray in his hair.

After Ruth came along, he no longer seemed to want to spend time alone with me. If I proposed lunch, he'd always say, "Let me see if Ruth is free then." I liked Ruth, and liked to be with her, but I missed being his special girl.

It took Ruth awhile to realize how profoundly the war had affected him. She noticed his exaggerated startle response, and she was as nervous as we had been waking him up. She said:

> To wake him up in the mornings I'd sing to him, but I wasn't about to touch him, because sometimes he'd have a strong reaction. His arms would flail out. I would probably have been struck without his realizing it. And when we'd watch the *NewsHour with Jim Lehrer* and they would put on the soldiers' pictures—those who had died—you could not talk to him. He just sat in silence out of respect. It really bothered him that these kids were dying.

But there were ways the war experience deepened his confidence in himself and made him feel nothing else could hurt him. Ruth saw some positive effects. Once they drove to the beach at Fenwick Island, Delaware, only to find she'd forgotten her suitcase, and they had to drive all the way back to McLean. She couldn't believe he wasn't angry with her. "That was so stupid of me," she said. "But he didn't have a word of impatience with me. He said, 'After you've been through a war, this sort of thing doesn't bother you.' "

Ruth once told Marty and me, "Your father was so . . . flexible." At that, we burst out laughing. "You knew a different man than the one we grew up with," we said. "Flexible? Nooo." He was fundamentally the same—values, principles, sense of humor, intellect—but energetically different: flexible versus uptight.

But by then we could see that the man who'd written "Tight, tight, tight, and down, down, down" in his wartime journal about combat, and who'd lived that way for so long, was peeking over the ridge and risking entering the line of fire once again—emotionally. At his age, he wrote love notes to Ruth, and in the safety of darkness, recounted his war stories to her. The emotional trust he placed in her still astounds me.

Some of his war stories concerned boot camp and his frustration at learning to use a rifle. When he fired, the rifle hit him in the cheek because he'd held it wrong. One of the other men helped him correct his position. He also told her about the lack of sleep, the cold, and the fear during combat; about their feet, always wet and chilled; about a soldier's need to be ever watchful; and about how men stuttered out of terror and anxiety. Ruth said:

> Bill wasn't a man who spoke a lot about the war, but at night sometimes he talked for hours. One time, I fell asleep after a while, and the next morning he said, "You didn't hear the end of . . ." I felt so guilty because it mattered so much to him. I got used to being awake at that time, listening.

He told her that no one who had not shared the bonds formed in battle could really understand what it was like.

> When he got the newsletter from the 80th Infantry Division, he always looked up his company to read about it. I never asked him why he didn't attend the reunions. When you think about it, in his life he'd rarely taken a vacation, and worked so hard at the paper, so going to a reunion with his schedule and a family might have been impossible. Or, truthfully, maybe it would have meant triggering painful memories.

Once, during an Easter Sunday brunch with friends, Dad had a flashback. He and Ruth were sipping a final cup of coffee when Dad suddenly got a strange look. "He got up from his chair," Ruth said, "and looked at me in an odd way. When we got outside to the car, I asked what had happened."

"All of a sudden," he told her in a low voice, "I felt like someone was shooting at me." Nearly sixty years had gone by since anyone actually had, but the flashback was powerful and unshakeable, even on a peaceful Easter morning. "It was like I was back there," he said.

The war that waged within for so many years was still going on, but with Ruth's help, Dad found that peace was at hand.

NOTES

1. Dana Priest and Anne Hull, "The War Inside: Troops Are Returning from the Battlefield with Psychological Wounds, but the Mental-Health System That Serves Them Makes Healing Difficult," *Washington Post*, June 17, 2007, p. A7.

2. Ernie Pyle, *Brave Men* (New York: Henry Holt, 1944), p. 491.

3. Scott Turow, interviewed by Charlie Rose, *Charlie Rose*, PBS, November 8, 2005.

CHAPTER SEVEN

The Gift of the Box

"The war was over for them. They weren't cold any more."
—Private Harold Lindstrom,
seeing dead German soldiers at the Battle of the Bulge

Dad watched as the nurse at the Army hospital in England examined the deep wound in his arm. The bullet had removed nearly all the flesh above the bone, exposing the extensor tendons. Finally, after two months in the hospital, he could bend his wrist without wincing in terrible pain. By moving his wrist up and down, he could shift the tendons back and forth in his forearm "like railroad trains," he recalled. The "railroad" entertained him while he spent the Christmas of 1944 in the hospital.

He'd been hit by a sniper at about 8 A.M. on November 8 in Rouves, France, and taken by ambulance to a hospital in Nancy overnight. After a brief stop at a Paris hospital, he was carried by hospital ship across the English Channel. By the time he got to England, the wound had become infected and his medical condition was more precarious.

Between the infections and the size of the wound, Dad's recuperation took several months. Of course, the war went on without him and without so many others who'd been wounded, killed, or captured. Because his war journal leaves off at the point where he was wounded in November and was never taken up again, I've had to piece together the progress of the Third Army's 80th Division—described in this chapter—from unit histories, *After Action Reports*, *Morning Reports*, interviews, and books.

• • •

The Third Army's offensive was running out of steam toward the last days of November 1944, mostly as a result of the shortage of men in all of General Patton's infantry units. The casualty lists for November were horrific: 1,049 killed, wounded, or missing in action for the 318th Regiment alone. The casualty totals for October were 556; for December, 620.

Combat fatigue also resulted in a serious loss of fighting troops, especially infantry. It was particularly prevalent among poorly trained, newly arrived replacements. Together with trench foot, combat fatigue represented a huge drain on Allied fighting manpower.

By this time in the war, perhaps more than four of every five infantrymen in combat were replacements. Lieutenant George Wilson, commanding officer of a rifle company fighting the Battle of the Bulge, received 100 replacements on December 29, 1944. "We discovered that these men had been on the rifle range only once," he said. "They had never thrown a grenade or fired a bazooka, mortar, or machine gun."[1] The Army's replacement system chose quantity over quality; thousands of eighteen- to twenty-year-olds were placed on the front lines, and many of them became casualties within only a few days. Paul Fussell, in his book *Wartime: Understanding and Behavior in the Second World War*, points out that for most soldiers and officers, war was on-the-job training.

On November 9, 1944—the day after Dad was shot near the Seille River and evacuated—the battle-tested 80th Division pushed forward to face the Delme Ridge, a mountaintop plateau. Taking the ridge was one of Patton's most important objectives. The 80th continued moving forward, averaging twelve and a half miles per day of combat. Finally, on December 7, the division rested near St. Avold, France, after having been in continuous contact with the enemy for 102 days.

The division left its rest area on December 18 to move southeast. The Germans had surrendered Metz (a city near Luxembourg and western Germany, which the Germans had occupied since 1940), allowing the Allies an opportunity to drive hard into Germany toward the Siegfried Line. But suddenly, the Germans launched a major counteroffensive, gambling all they had and breaking through in the Ardennes, a region of dense forests and rolling hills located primarily in Belgium and Luxembourg. Consequently, orders came for the 80th to switch directions and head north to the city of Luxembourg from the area around Metz, and then to seize a stretch of supply road from Trier, Germany to Bastogne, Belgium. The German advance into Belgium and the bitter conflict that ensued later became known as the infamous "Battle of the Bulge."

American troops from the 101st Airborne Division had entered Bastogne on December 19 and soon found themselves trapped. The Wehrmacht (German forces) surrounded the town and isolated it, while 30,000 U.S. Third Army troops slogged through the snow, sleet, dense fog, and mud to reach the town. Ultimately, more than 1 million men fought in this battle: 600,000 Americans, 50,000 British, and 500,000 Germans. The battle lasted forty days and extended over the most frigid winter Europe had seen in fifty years.

Vital to the success of the German penetration was the taking of Bastogne. If Nazi forces could capture this vital communications center, they would be able to fan out along an excellent road network, but if they failed, they'd be forced to advance along limited and vulnerable supply arteries or make a complete withdrawal.

The 318th Infantry Regiment boarded trucks as darkness fell on Christmas Eve in order to help the 4th Armored Division break the encirclement of Bastogne. Low on ammunition from recent battles, the trapped 101st Airborne Division desperately needed relief.

The 2nd Battalion of the 318th fought through fierce enemy artillery, mortar, and automatic weapon fire, not to mention cold rains and snow. After bitter fighting and heavy casualties, the Battalion reached the woods near Hompre, outside the Bastogne perimeter, reducing the distance between the Americans and Germans to 4,000 yards. The Americans were impatient and anxious to connect with the isolated 101st.

"We expect to contact the 101st Airborne soon," Captain P. W. Foreman told Lieutenant Walter Carr, second in command of 318-E Company. These small patrols could be nerve-wracking ordeals for those required to creep in darkness across the countryside, not knowing if they would trip a mine or set off a flare that would expose them, but Carr seemed to thrive on them. Captain Foreman said, "We need to know what their exact positions are so we don't shoot at each other [when we approach]."

Captured German soldiers told Lieutenant Carr that they used red and green flashes at night as recognition signals between units. But being seen by the enemy as his patrol stole through the dense wooded hostile territory might not have been Carr's only problem. He also worried that the American Airborne troops might shoot at anything that moved. Carr improvised camouflage clothing from white parachutes to blend with the snow on the ground, then he guided three other men in the patrol in the harsh, cold morning hours of December 27 to infiltrate active enemy machine gun positions. In a stroke of luck, the patrol ran into American tanks from the 26th Engineer Battalion and hitched a ride into the interior of Bastogne.

After securing vital information from the headquarters of the besieged troops, they returned to the Battalion with an overlay of the positions inside the circle. They arrived back at headquarters in time to participate in the morning's attack, led by the tanks of the 4th Armored Division.

"They did everything but kiss, they were so damn glad [to see us]," Carr said later. "I told them how the relieving forces were progressing. I felt like a GI Santa Claus." For this action, Carr was awarded his second Silver Star, and several of the men in the patrol received Bronze Stars. The 318th Regiment also received the Presidential Unit Citation—the nation's highest award to a military unit—for liberating the 101st.

The Germans had initiated their fierce counterattack against the invading Allied forces on December 16 and had driven westward into Luxembourg and Belgium, employing as many as fifteen divisions, with artillery and tank support. During the entire month of January 1945, unit reports say, "the weather remained below freezing, the ground covered with snow and ice, which considerably increased the difficulty of operations, whether offensive or defensive." The dominating cold caused terrible suffering. Temperatures ranged from 0° to -10° Fahrenheit.

In his book *Citizen Soldiers*, Stephen Ambrose tells of an AA gunner attached to the 4th Armored Division who recalled, "I was on due guard [up next for duty] and went out to my half track to relieve the man on guard. He couldn't get out of the gun turret. His overcoat was wet when he got in and it froze so he couldn't get out." In addition, Private Patrick Stewart of 318-E remembers settling into his foxhole for the night with wet socks on. "You'd take off your wet socks and pin them under your armpits to dry overnight in between your shirt and your coat. Then you'd put on your other socks—the dry ones. You can't imagine the feeling of putting on those dry socks."

GI Harold Lindstrom thought constantly about how cold he was. When he saw his first dead Germans, he envied their peace of mind and body. "The war was over for them," Lindstrom said. "They weren't cold any more."[2]

According to *After Action Reports* for the 318th, morale hit an all-time low during January: "An epidemic of self-inflicted wounds occurred during the period 1 January to 15 January [19]45. It is my opinion the indirect cause was due to excessive fatigue, cold weather and heavy enemy shelling."

The German counteroffensive stopped after six weeks, at the end of which their casualties reached 100,000 dead, wounded, or captured. The greatest American losses of the entire war were in the Battle of the Bulge—80,987 casualties, including some 19,000 killed in action. It would be early spring before things began to look up for the Allied armies.

February 1945 brought the melting of the snow, a welcome sign, but with it came a gruesome unveiling. Now visible were the bodies of many dead Germans, as well as cattle, pigs, and horses scattered throughout the countryside.

●　　●　　●

Lieutenant Carr told me that my father was the kind of officer men could count on to show emotional stability and calm in battle. Michael Doubler, in his book *Closing with the Enemy: How GIs Fought the War in Europe, 1944–1945*, said that troops wanted their captains and lieutenants to have a temperament with an even keel and self-control. "An excitable officer was ineffective. Officers learned that speaking in a calm, firm voice during tense situations was the best way to reassure soldiers."

Platoon commanders bore the brunt of officer casualties and were difficult to replace. So Captain Paul Chmar, the E Company commander, must have been glad to see Dad return to duty on February 4, 1945, after nearly three months in the hospital and rehabilitation. Dad was back with his company just in time for the terrible and bitter battle for control of the Sauer River in Luxembourg.

On February 7, the 318th Regiment began its assault on the Siegfried Line, but the natural barrier of the Sauer River that fell between the Regiment and the Siegfried Line had to be crossed first. Breaching the Siegfried Line held great psychological significance for the GIs. Rumors about the strength of the Line flourished well in advance. The Siegfried Line—whose construction was begun by Adolf Hitler in 1937—was a powerful system stretching nearly 390 miles of concrete forts organized to form a deep and formidable zone of defense. The Line usually consisted of five rows of pyramid-shaped, reinforced concrete projections ("dragon teeth") sitting on a concrete mat, sunk three or four feet into the ground.

All along the Line, the Germans resisted with machine guns, mortar, and artillery. The 318th crossed the Sauer despite flood-stage waters filled with debris and a swift current of fifteen miles per hour, but E and G Companies had trouble initially getting their boats into the water. Clayton Warman of F Company told me in an interview:

> We crossed in the middle of the night when the river was high. Some of the boats overturned and men were drowned. It was brutal. I remember a couple of the platoons in E Company never made it; they came across in daylight and got blasted out of the water. This was one of the worst experiences of the war, with the cold, the snow, the mud, and the very swift, very high, river.

Both sides had wearied of the hard winter, the wounds, the deprivation, and the death. Their state of mind was reflected in the words of some captured German POWs, who said they held out no hope for winning the war, and they thought that the clock had reached "five minutes before twelve."[3]

Ernie Pyle ably articulated the American infantrymen's thoughts:

> The worst experience . . . is just the accumulated blur, and the hurting vagueness of being too long in the lines, the everlasting alertness, the noise and fear, the cell-by-cell exhaustion, the thinning of the surrounding ranks as day follows nameless day. And the constant march into eternity of one's own small quota of chances for survival.[4]

Pyle understood the value of the infantry and the sacrifices they made:

> . . . the God-damned infantry, as they like to call themselves. I love the infantry because they are the underdogs. They are the mud-rain-frost-and-wind boys. They have no comforts, and they even learn to do without the necessities. And in the end they are the guys that wars can't be won without.[5]

•   •   •

February, though not quite as cold, was nearly as miserable as January because of the incessant rainfall, the scarcity of food, and an epidemic of diarrhea. The weather rendered the roads nearly useless. Nevertheless, unit reports said:

> From 7–14 Feb 318th Inf virtually blasted its way inside the Siegfried Line to a depth of over two miles. Despite the fact that the enemy morale in all ranks was noticeably lower than

ever before encountered, the very nature of the terrain and well prepared defenses tended to make an offensive operation difficult and slow. One delaying measure always used extensively by retreating Germans, the planting of mines and booby traps, was found to have been employed by them in this particular area on an even larger scale. Roads and ditches supposedly cleared of mines were found to contain others that had remained undetected.

Morning Reports show Dad, on February 20, going from duty to "sk (LD)"—meaning "sick, line of duty"—and "lost to 101st Evac Hosp," but the reports don't say for how long. Since he had not been wounded again, perhaps his arm wound troubled him or the infection had recurred.

Dad then rejoined his unit and in March the 2nd Battalion of the 318th swept into the Rhine Valley and faced the last natural barrier to their drive: the Rhine River. But first they had to fight their way through the town of Weiskirchen. Captain Chmar led the Battalion into the town, where the battle raged for several days with house-to-house fighting against SS troops of the 6th Mountain Division. On March 17, finally, Weiskirchen was taken and the Germans were spun back to the Rhine River. Chmar received the Distinguished Service Cross for his leadership.

The Division continued its drive through this beautiful region of Germany, land of Hansel and Gretel. Occasionally stopping for training, the men set up roadblocks, established bridgeheads, and repaired bridges. Sometimes traveling on foot, sometimes by trucks and jeeps, they cleared out pockets of the enemy and collected prisoners of war.

In Kassel, the 80th Division seized the Nazis' largest military medical supply depot, more than $100,000 worth of new surgical instruments and vast stores of pharmaceutical supplies. After more bitter house-to-house fighting, they captured the city.

On April 21, the Division was ordered into Nuremberg for guard duty to relieve 3rd Infantry Division, XXI Corps. Enduring more icy wind and bitter cold, they patrolled the city and rounded up displaced persons who'd been liberated from either concentration camps or slave labor camps. Nuremberg is also where Dad got several of his wartime souvenirs—a large Nazi flag and two copper swastikas with bullet holes in them that he ripped off the wall of the famous Zeppelin Stadium, where Hitler delivered many of his fiery, demagogic speeches.

They departed Nuremberg on April 28, crossed the Danube River, and arrived at Hofling, preparing to follow the 13th Armored Division across the Austrian border. German soldiers, sensing the end of the war was near, poured in and surrendered by the thousands. Hitler was reportedly incensed that his troops were surrendering.

The frigid, wet weather continued as the GIs crossed the Isar River in assault boats, but no shots were fired. News reached them that Adolf Hitler and his wife, Eva Braun, had died by their own hands on April 30. Hitler had put a gun to his mouth and pulled the trigger, while Braun swallowed a vial of poison.

Earlier that spring, Hitler had threatened to kill all the Allied POWs. But on May 1, the day after his death, Germany agreed to leave Allied prisoners of war in the POW camps that the Germans had abandoned as the Allies advanced. He argued that if the Nazis killed their Allied prisoners, Allies who, in turn, held German POWs would retaliate with brutal treatment of their own. Hitler was afraid this would eliminate surrender as an attractive option for the German soldier. He found the Geneva Convention a nasty inconvenience, saying, "We should scrap the idiotic thing."

German resistance lightened by the beginning of May, and the war would soon be over. Members of the Wehrmacht continued to stream down from the mountains and give up, highly motivated to surrender to the American forces rather than the Russians. The history between the Russian and the German armies reflected mutual savagery and cruelty. German barbarity in Russia dating back to 1941 was well-known to the Russian soldiers, many of whom looked forward to their retribution in Germany. According to Max Hastings in his book *Armageddon: The Battle for Germany, 1944–1945*: "The orgy of looting, destruction and rape which followed the Red Army's triumph in Berlin and across the rest of eastern Germany seemed to [Russian leader Joseph] Stalin a just recompense to his soldiers for their labour, and a fitting chastisement for the German people." The 2nd Battalion crossed the border from Germany to Austria and reached Braunau, the birthplace of Adolf Hitler, where they overtook the 13th Armored Division. But first another river needed to be navigated. Some soldiers crossed the Inn River in assault boats, but some had to cross on a "narrow, rickety, partially destroyed railroad bridge, awash in the swift Inn River. Crossing the bridge had to be done in a single column of men and could only be negotiated with the greatest difficulty, due to the slipperiness of the bank and swift current," according to Robert Murrell in *The Blue Ridge Division Answers the Call in WWII*.

The 318th Regiment operated its last tactical Command Post of the war out of the house in which Hitler was born. The 13th Armored and the 80th Infantry Divisions jointly agreed to make a survey of the food stocks in Braunau. There they found a shocking 12,000 POWs and forced laborers, 4,000 of whom were Americans.

The Americans, mostly airmen from Eighth Army Air Corps, had recently arrived after an eighteen-day march under German guard from their POW camp at Stalag XVII-B near Krems, Austria. "We bypassed the city of Braunau on our last day of the march and went south along the river for perhaps ten miles, until reaching a large 'national forest' where we were told to settle in and do the best we could to survive," says Ned Handy, who was a prisoner at Stalag XVII-B. (The prison was later made famous by the Billy Wilder movie *Stalag 17* in 1953, starring William Holden.) The men were left in the forest, with an ever decreasing number of German guards milling around, for about a week, until the 13th Armored Division freed them just before the 318th arrived.

Labor camps in and around Braunau held the remaining detainees, nearly all of whom had been forced into the Austrian camps from other European countries. At least 250 French prisoners were housed near the aluminum factory where they were put to work. Since many survived on subsistence rations, the 318th Infantry Regiment and the 13th Armored Division worked together to provide them with medical treatment and food.

Private Paul Mercer, a soldier in the 318th from New Hampshire, remembers seeing two prison camps around Braunau: the one that held American airmen, and the other a slave labor camp. The latter held the workers overnight, and then in the morning farmers would come for them or they would go to work in a factory or on the road. "The camp was a bunch of bare barracks," said Mercer in an interview with me:

> . . . and barbed wire, of course. There were French, Polish, German, and Italian. We had to sort them out so we could send them back to their home country. They were terrified of us and didn't know if we were going to kill them or what. Our job was to get the names of their towns and their families. They were no threat to the Reich, they were just people the Germans picked up, young and strong, teenage up to age thirty.

Some French prisoners invited Private Stewart and some other enlisted men to their barracks. The stark rooms were sparsely furnished; each prisoner could keep only a few belongings. One of the Frenchmen, in a festive mood, suddenly popped a paper bag, and the American soldiers, fresh from combat, dived for the floor. The Frenchman quickly apologized.

The GIs made a wonderful discovery in Braunau: crate upon crate of fresh eggs. Stewart found wooden crates of 500 eggs each and took two of the crates to his company. He cooked a twelve-egg omelet for each man on the cast-iron stove in the kitchen of the house where they stayed. "I made one for Bill, one for Berti . . . I put cheese from the K-rations into the omelets," he recalled. Legend has it that one liberated Canadian pilot ate twenty-seven eggs at one sitting.

When the soldiers entered the camps to process and care for the forced laborers, they were mobbed by men trying to communicate in any of five or six different languages. Dad met one Frenchman who worked in the aluminum factory. I tried to imagine the meeting of the two young men: Dad, a war-weary American Army officer glad to put his French to good use, and the Frenchman, ecstatic to see his day of freedom arrive, hoping it meant he would soon reunite with his family. Perhaps they shook hands, greeting each other in French, each asking the other where he was from. The Frenchman might have asked about the progress of the war and smiled when Dad told him the Germans were surrendering in droves and that things looked good for an end to it. Maybe they even exchanged pictures of wives and children.

Then the prisoner may have thought to give Dad something. Going back to his bunk, maybe he bent down underneath it to where he kept his private belongings and pulled out his gift. The gift was a box that measured about the length and width of a letter-sized piece of paper and about three inches in depth. The prisoner handed it to him, perhaps shyly. He told Dad he'd made the box himself out of aluminum from the factory where he worked. He'd engraved on the top a picture of the heads of a man and a woman with a design of ivy or flowers around the edge. On the side of the box he had written "Braunau 1944." The box worked on hinges, and the top closed neatly. Even though it was fairly large, Dad knew instantly that he'd find room for it in his knapsack.

The war souvenirs Dad had gathered up to that point, the Nazi flag and the swastikas from Nuremberg, were mementos from Hitler's savage reign. But the box symbolized hope and friendship. Dad grew up believing in the ideal of freedom, and he still believed, but sometimes he wondered what all the killing was for and what it would accomplish in the long run. Now he had something tangible that he could keep and touch to remind him of the friend he made in Braunau—a man who had been locked behind barbed wire only a day before they had met. Out of this terrible experience, the man had created something lovely with his own hands. Did he treasure it above all his meager possessions at the camp? Had he planned to give the box to his wife or his mother when he finally got home? Instead, he gave it away—to an American soldier. I wonder if he knew how much the box meant to my father and how Dad would cherish it for the rest of his life.

• • •

The Regiment left Braunau on May 6, a day that dawned bright, clear, and cool. The 318th Infantry had a new assignment: to assemble and arrange for the discharge of the German Sixth Army. Negotiations for surrender by its commander, General der Panzer Truppe Balck, to Major General Horace L. McBride, commanding general of the 80th Division, were complete. The war in Europe was all but officially over. As previously stated, the Germans had good reason to surrender to the United States.

According to the unit reports: "The German Army Commander's underlying reason for negotiating this surrender was to prevent their capture by the Russians, in whose territory they actually were located at the time."

"I was told that some German soldiers were so desperate to evade Russian capture that they tried to swim the frigid Enns River, which separated the Russian zone from the American zone, and they drowned," wrote Lieutenant Carr. [6]

"We laughed at the sight of a German officer who was frantically trying to surrender his company to our column as the trucks rumbled by," Lieutenant John Ingles wrote in his book *A Soldier's Passage*. While the Germans stood at attention with their weapons stacked neatly beside them, "the officer waved a white flag like a bullfighter at each passing truck. No one would even stop. Finally someone motioned him to start marching his company to the rear."

Trains brought E Company from Braunau eastward to the next Command Post at Schwanenstadt, Austria. Russians and Americans had orchestrated a meeting in Liezen, Austria, on Victory in Europe Day (V-E Day). The trucks to carry the men in his company on to Liezen wouldn't be available for several hours, so Lieutenant Carr, now serving as company commander, left with a small advance party in the company jeep to be ready with instructions when the Company arrived. Other than Carr, the advance party consisted only of a sergeant, a driver, and a German-speaking member of E Company.

Carr chose the shortest route to Liezen, which took him by the resort village of Ebensee, located in the beautiful Salzkammergut region of Austria. They wound through snow-covered Alps and past well-cared for homes and farms, stopping in Ebensee to buy film at a photo shop. For some reason, the proprietor had prominently displayed photos taken at a concentration camp, showing the emaciated bodies of inmates being piled onto a large flatbed trailer. Carr, shocked at what he saw in the photos, insisted the group go to the camp. Before that, he hadn't been aware that there was such a camp in Ebensee.

They worked their way up toward the base of the mountains, where U.S. soldiers now stood at the camp's gate. Their disbelieving eyes rested on inmates wearing black and white striped uniforms. The smell of the dead and dying hit their nostrils and sickened them. Carr observed that the bodies lying around had "not yet begun to bloat," suggesting that the liberating American soldiers had arrived very recently. General Patton, he learned, had ordered the townspeople to come to the camp, he said, "to see and smell the atrocities Hitler's henchmen had committed."

After about thirty minutes, Carr's party left and continued on the narrow roads to Liezen, lined with long columns of fully armed Germans. The lieutenant later described the scene:

> They looked very little like the defeated army they were supposed to be. Many of them had burp guns or rifles slung over their shoulders and were lugging potato masher grenades on their belts. But they did have the look of defeat on their faces as they silently and sullenly gazed at us, probably the first American soldiers they had ever seen.

Carr tried to stop the German soldiers from using the Nazi salute. Outnumbered by the thousands, he failed. As he later told me, the drive down to Liezen was difficult:

> There was no doubt whatsoever who was in charge: They were, if they wanted to be. The four of us had no way of disarming a 122,000-man German army, and we acted accordingly. Our driver needed no coaching to veer our jeep off the road, which was one lane in many spots, to clear out of the German column's way. At any moment I knew a rogue group—four or five—that was tired of walking could easily open up on us with

their weapons if they wanted to commandeer our jeep. No one would ever suspect murder. They already had in their column some American jeeps captured from the Russians, who got them through our Lend-Lease program. I constantly feared this scenario as our jeep bucked their column mile after mile. We knew the gravity of the situation and watched them in silence. We knew we had the authority to tell them what to do, but we also knew that would be stupid.

When Carr saw Dad in Liezen, he recounted the horrors he'd seen at Ebensee. But they had no time to dwell on it because they had an observance to prepare for. The war in Europe had ended at long last, and V-E Day had arrived. In a somber ceremony under a brilliant blue sky, the Americans marched from their side of the bridge over the Enns River toward the Russians coming from their territory on the opposite side. When they met, they raised both flags and planted them together in the middle. This historic meeting was toasted by the raising of many glasses of vodka, and Dad was elected the "designated vodka drinker" for E Company. He was also interviewed by a reporter from the Russian newspaper *Izvestia*, a task he relished. They found a drink for the reporter, who then offered the observation, "In Russia, when we have something to drink we like to have a little something to eat." So they rummaged around and found one last box of rations to share.

Generals Walton Walker and McBride shared toasts with the Russian general. Lieutenant Carr and my father had several photos taken together on this historic day. Dad's favorite, and mine, shows the two of them standing arm in arm with (and head and shoulders above) a ragtag group of Russian soldiers.

Soon, orders came to speed up movement of the retreating Germans from Liezen to the U.S. Prisoner of War collection point at Moosbach, eighty-five miles to the northwest. Thousands of German prisoners awaited processing.

Dad wrote a letter to his two-year-old nephew, Frankie Dwyer, Jr., enclosing a photo taken the week before in Braunau with the newly liberated French captives:

Dear Frankie,

Probably until you saw the enclosed snapshot you had no idea your Uncle Bill was such a sourpuss. The Frenchmen weren't very happy because they thought they'd be able to scoot home on V-E Day (U.S. and Russian military needs had to come first so they were held up for a while). The surrender of the German Army, once an outstanding fighting force, was a tremendous spectacle. First and last columns of trucks of every conceivable type, German jeeps and autos, then carts and horses and finally those who could find no other way. Often there were just four of us among thousands of Germans and I can assure you that my confident attitude was not very deep-rooted especially in the midst of groups that had not turned in their small arms. Now they are bivouacked on the Austrian plain and from any point this Army, mighty even in defeat, stretches as far as the eye (corrected to 20/20) can see. At present we are busy getting reorganized and after that *je ne sais pas*. The Jap war has priority, especially for officers, so I don't have much hope of getting to see you very soon. Send my regards to your Daddy when you write and give my love to your Mama. I'm sending an SS knife to your grandma, and your Mama can use it to slice your spinach. Love to all at home. Love, Uncle Bill.

As Dad marched through Austria, he contemplated the sight of the vast and once potent German army. Columns of re-treating soldiers stretched endlessly across the valley. He told Ruth later that as he watched, in his mind he heard the hymn from Act Three of Wagner's opera *Tannhäuser*, where the re-turning pilgrims begin to sing. Their soft voices strengthen as they draw closer, thanking God for forgiveness and expressing regret for the evil deeds they have committed:

By atonement and repentance I have made my peace
With the Lord, to whom my heart bows down,
Who has crowned my remorse with blessing,
The Lord to whom I raise my song.

The pilgrims pass by and slowly move across the valley. Their chorus swells, gradually increasing in power until it reaches a crescendo, in an almost military cadence:

The grace of salvation is granted to the penitent,
who shall enter into the peace of heaven!
Hell and death cannot affright him,
therefore will I praise God all the days of my life.
Hallelujah, hallelujah for evermore!

NOTES

1. Stephen E. Ambrose, *Citizen Soldiers: The U.S. Army from the Normandy Beaches to the Bulge to the Surrender of Germany, June 7, 1944, to May 7, 1945* (New York: Simon & Schuster, 1997), p. 276.

2. Max Hastings, *Armageddon: The Battle for Germany 1944-1945* (New York: Alfred A. Knopf, 2004), p. 227.

3. Michael D. Doubler, *Closing with the Enemy: How GIs Fought the War in Europe, 1944-1945* (Lawrence, Kans.: University Press of Kansas, 1994).

4. Ernie Pyle, *Brave Men* (New York: Henry Holt, 1944), p. 477.

5. http://journalism.indiana.edu/resources/erniepyle/wartime-columns/.

6. Walter P. Carr, unpublished manuscript.

Dad's family in England about 1923. At the top are my grandmother, Annie Watt Davidson Elvin, and my grandfather, William John "Jim" Elvin. At the bottom, from left, are Georgie, Kay, and Bill (my Dad). Dad's younger sister, Mary, had not been born yet.

My parents, Jane and Bill Elvin, in 1942, the year after they got married.

Bill Elvin in uniform.

Dad in uniform in early 1944, before he went overseas.

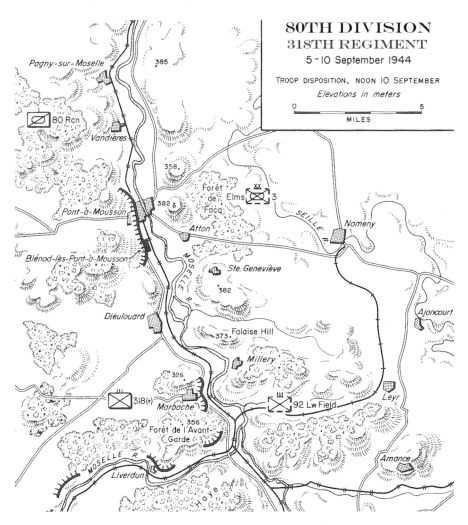

A map of the 318th Regiment's operations along the Moselle River and Canal in September 1944. U.S. ARMY PHOTO.

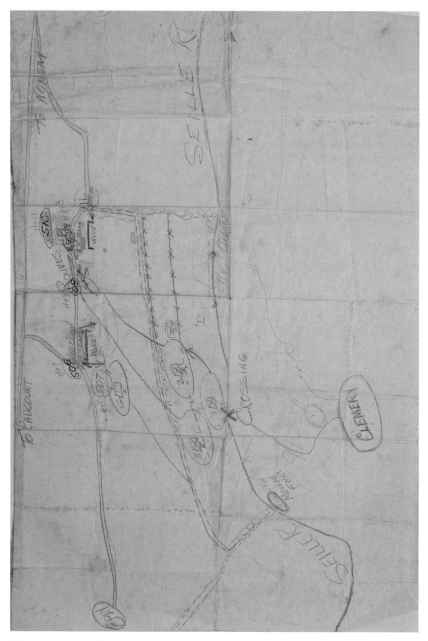

The map Dad drew for reconnaissance purposes before the attack on Rouves on November 8, 1944. Dad was shot and wounded on the day of the attack.

My father is shown on the left with a group of French forced laborers in May 1945. The men had been liberated by U.S. soldiers from a camp in Austria.

Meeting the Russian soldiers at the Enns River in Liezen, Austria, on V-E Day, May 8, 1945. Lieutenant Walter Carr is the tall American near the left, while Dad is the tall American toward the right.

Three prisoners at the Ebensee concentration camp days after its liberation on May 6, 1945. They are eating sugar cubes, since they were unable to digest food after starving for so long. NATIONAL ARCHIVES (III-SC-208003)

Dad as company commander in Kempten, Germany, after the war in Europe had ended. He is standing in front of the F Company Command Post.

Another photo of Dad as the company commander of F Company in Kempten, Germany, in the summer of 1945.

Dad inspecting F Company weapons in Pilsen, Czechoslovakia, in October 1945.
PHOTO COURTESY GEORGE ANDERSON.

Dad and me at Deep Creek Lake in Western Maryland in 1949. I'm wearing my red tennis shoes, which Dad rescued when one of them landed in the lake.

The Elvin family celebrating my brother George's second birthday in 1960. From left, me, Marty, George, Jay, and Dad. This is one of the few photos of all four of us children together.

Dad at work at the newspaper in 1959. PHOTO BY BILL HOLLINGER.

The Elvins at the McLean Family Restaurant around 1995. Seated clockwise around the table are: me (in front), Dad, Ruth, Molly, Ben and my husband Al. Standing behind are Marty and George.

Polish survivors of the camp at Ebensee commemorating the sixtieth
anniversary of its liberation in May 2005.

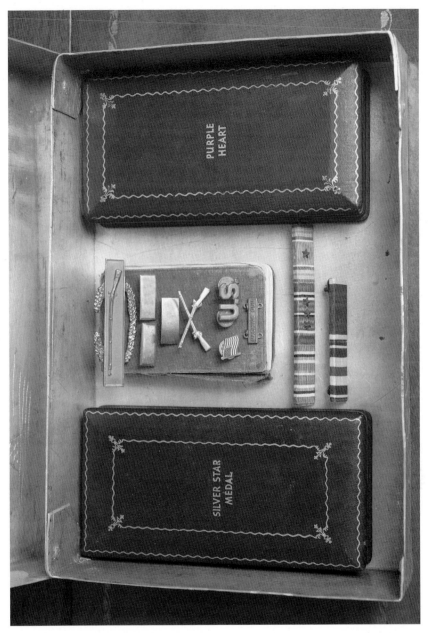

The box given to Dad by the prisoner at Braunau held Dad's Silver Star, Purple Heart, Combat Infantry Badge, and childhood Bible. Photo by Bill Hollinger.

The side of the box, where the prisoner who made it etched "1944 Braunau." Photo by Bill Hollinger.

The top of the box from Braunau, showing the drawing of a man and a woman surrounded by flowers. Photo by Bill Hollinger.

CHAPTER EIGHT

The Unbroken Circle

"You have to dig deep to bury your father."
—Roma proverb

"He didn't talk about it in daylight, but in the dark," Ruth said. "It reminded me of *Cold Mountain*, and I remember thinking how important it is for people to tell their story: the story of the war and what had happened to him and the other men."

The shooting may stop, but for a soldier, war never ends. Memories can weigh on a combat veteran more heavily than any military-issue rucksack or body armor. It would have been good for my family to know that it was better to deal with my father's wounded emotions before they were pushed aside and made unconscious—before they became almost too deeply buried to call back.

Dad never sought treatment despite his disturbing memories and nightmares. He didn't attribute any difficulties with his family or his problems with anger and nervousness to the war and his resulting PTSD, and he never discussed the emotional effects of his wartime experiences. Many years after the fact, however, he felt safe enough with Ruth to let some of the memories bubble to the surface.

On Fathers' Day 2001, writer Anne Taylor Fleming spoke to *The NewsHour with Jim Lehrer* and described her father when he returned from World War II: "The era, the ethos, the uniform of stiff upper-lip masculinity defined everything about him. He expected to be in charge, to preside over and provide for his family. These were the father-knows-best dads and we were their Kittens." Her words could have described our family as well.

Upon their return from the war, these men were seen as heroes, so how did they go on to live regular lives? Dad was a typical World War II combat vet, a product of his era. It was not his style to reveal his anxieties. He had a strong sense of propriety and discretion, like most of his generation. Traumatized as they were, in hell for months at a time, they were not going to inflict their painful memories on the people they loved.

The returning World War II soldier was caught in a bind. As Stephen Ambrose says, the most extreme experience a human being can go through is to serve as a combat infantryman, yet according to Mark D. Van Ells, author of *To Hear Only Thunder Again: America's World War II Veterans Come Home*, "To be effective in combat, soldiers must learn to suppress the feelings it generates." The returning veteran's intimate knowledge of military combat and its hardships sometimes separated him from the very civilian society he had loved, served, and defended. As Guy Kelnhofer, a Pacific war veteran, said, "We can love our wives and children. We can give them loyalty and devotion. But there is a part of us that will always remain detached and apart."[1]

The idyllic life at home that a veteran may have imagined during the war was simply not there upon his return. "Many guys who had been looking forward so long to a release from the bureaucracy and restraints of the Army had forgotten that civilian life also has its bureaucrats and its drawbacks," said Bill

Mauldin, creator of the cartoon characters Willie and Joe, so beloved by GIs during the war.[2]

Most veterans' families and other civilians hoped the vets would put the past behind them and get on with their lives, but it wasn't easy. The long-term separation from friends and family left many veterans lonely and with no one to share what they'd been through. Upon returning home, Dad must have reconnected with his old friend Norval Graham, who had been so seriously wounded, but he never mentioned what became of him.

It was hard to talk about having been through hell without sounding like a complainer, but good soldiers did not complain about what they had gone through. Complaining would have been disrespectful for those whose lives had been lost.

"Most war heroes don't feel brave or heroic at the time, but they do their duty, despite often feeling overwhelmed and horrified, in order to protect others," says a fact sheet from the U.S. Department of Veterans Affairs. Yet when they returned, they were treated as heroes—a designation many felt they didn't deserve no matter how bravely they had performed in battle. In fact, you will often hear a veteran say, "The real heroes are the ones who died."

All combat veterans dealt with survivor guilt upon return to the States. Moritz Thomsen, who served as a bombardier during World War II, remembers, "To move back into that society that could dance, sing and rush into life with the enthusiasm of puppies seemed like a betrayal of the millions dead."[3]

Before World War II, the military relied heavily on psychological screening to weed out men at risk for emotional or mental breakdowns from combat exposure. But the war ended with the military rejecting the efficacy of screening, conceding that "every man has his breaking point." At that point, the concept of stress as a psychophysiological reality became part of the understanding of the consequences of combat. Psychologists believed that a soldier's difficulty in recovering from the trauma of war was not inborn, like bipolar disorder or schizophrenia, but the result of too much exposure to combat.

"One way of thinking about PTSD is that it's not a problem of remembering; it's that we're unable to forget," says Dr. Robert Ursano.[4] "PTSD is actually a disorder of forgetting."

Dad regained his solid emotional footing later in life—an accomplishment he may have shared with other combat vets. Research shows that combat veterans, especially veterans of heavy combat, while at greater risk of emotional and behavioral problems in the postwar years, became more resilient and less helpless over time when compared to veterans of light combat or noncombatants. In addition, Dad's strong upbringing may have been another factor in his ability to succeed later in his life. Dad had been sustained during the war by the constant moral strength instilled in him by his parents and by the secure foundation the family provided him. He was relatively free of other stressors or psychiatric illness: Other than the early death of his brother Georgie, his childhood was happy. So while there was a childhood bereavement, the family support was there, and he was able to continue his pattern of success and achievement.

•   •   •

Further research has examined the experiences of children from families in which a father suffered PTSD from World War II combat experience. Although the impact varied among those studied, the legacy of wartime trauma was apparent in the adult lives of many of these offspring.

Today, we baby boomers want to understand our parents' stories on our own terms. We want to fill in the hole in the family history, knowing that the stories behind the silences have affected us. As writer Scott Turow said in an interview with

Charlie Rose in 2005, "The war experience seemed critical to understanding my father."

I've talked with many others whose fathers fought in World War II, and the story is always the same: He went as a young man, he fought, perhaps was wounded, and rarely spoke of it again. We were saturated with the glory of World War II, but not from our parents—from the culture.

My father's story is one that belongs to so many others. Nearly all World War II veterans see the war as the single greatest event in their lives, no matter what fame or success their postwar lives and careers brought. It strikes a universal chord among this fraternity of men.

I didn't do this research or write this book to look for accounts of courage or skeletons in my father's closet. I just wanted to understand him better. I knew what to admire about him before I began writing—and then I discovered his vulnerabilities and what he was up against in his life. And I found that, as Turow says, "A lot of things that I admired about my father were intensified." Dad wasn't a "bounce-on-the-knee" type of father or grandfather, but he took care of his family by being there for them and being loyal. No birthday or special event went by unmarked or unremembered. He showed up without ever insisting upon, or even welcoming, recognition for it.

His strong sense of loyalty was forged by his parents but was finely tuned during the war. Under the stress of combat, the brotherhood of combat infantrymen had to stick together to survive. As a platoon leader, Dad was not only responsible for the welfare of his men; he shared the awful realities of war with them every day and night.

He stuck by people, particularly when they were down on their luck. A friend of Dad's was sent to prison in 1972 for accepting bribes during the man's tenure on the Fairfax County Board of Supervisors. Even though they weren't particularly close, Dad kept up a correspondence with him while he served his time. Dad didn't care if people thought he was befriending someone "unworthy"; he just did it because the man needed a friend.

A neighbor of ours, "Herb" (not his real name), lived like a hermit alone in his house, where the holes in the floor enabled the raccoons to come inside. After the man lost his university teaching job, Dad gave him a job addressing newspapers. I remember Herb sitting at the old addressograph machine, shabbily dressed, cigarette dangling from his mouth, his yellowed fingers hitting the keys. After Herb went into a nursing home, Dad visited him and spent time each day on the phone with him, talking about local and national politics and keeping him company.

I also learned some other things about Dad in the course of writing this book that made me angry. Why didn't he share more of himself? Why didn't he ask more of us, his children? He had a huge retirement party in 1992 that was attended by many people from the community as well as from the old *Washington Star* whom he hadn't seen in years. I have no recollection of his telling me about the party, and when I came across mention of it in the newspaper, including quotes from him and others, I was upset. Looking at the date in the newspaper, I finally realized that it must have been the same week that my husband had a serious operation. Dad didn't want to trouble me.

He was the glue that held the community of McLean together, celebrating and communicating good things about the town. Warren Carmichael, the county police public information officer, knew him for thirty years. Carmichael said that Dad exemplified the idea of "a gentleman of the press. I regard him as someone with the highest of principles and integrity who is thoroughly committed to putting out a good community newspaper."

Dad was a tough interview himself—self-effacing and guarded with words. He was a good listener who preferred to ask the questions and who thought the subject of himself should be swiftly concluded.

With characteristic wry humor, Dad liked to say that the horrendous World War II battle of the Moselle River was reported by the *Washington Star* in one sentence: "The Third Army advanced against light resistance." Dad was unfailingly modest about his own achievements—like John F. Kennedy who, when asked how he became a hero, said, "It was involuntary. They sank my boat." When I asked Dad how he got the Silver Star (the third highest military decoration that can be awarded to a member of any branch of the U.S. Armed Forces, given for valor in the face of the enemy), he always said, "Oh, they just had to give out their quota that day."

Popular on the local speech circuit, in each talk he included some tidbits of history and personal anecdotes about well-known local people, always maintaining or at least restoring dignity. He told a joke about the infamously ugly Ingleside Building on Old Dominion Drive in McLean that went like this:

Q: Where do you get the best view of McLean?
A: *From the Ingleside Building.*
Q: Why do you say that?
A: *Because from inside, you can't see the Ingleside Building.*

But he never told a joke at anyone's expense. He ended that quip by saying that the owner had the last laugh when he sold the building for $9 million in 1986.

Dad knew all politics was local. He wrote about football teams, tax referenda, weddings, and huge vegetables grown in local gardens. He gave people what they wanted to know about their community. He appreciated the unintended compliment from a subscriber who wrote, "I really don't like your newspaper. I only subscribe for informational purposes."

You could always tell when he was talking on the phone to his dear friend George Lilly because the dry wit flew. They had lunch together every Thursday with a small group; invitations to join were much sought after.

But gradually, Dad's pulmonary fibrosis began to win the battle. He went to the Heart and Lung Transplant Center at Inova Fairfax Hospital in Falls Church, Virginia, and they quizzed him to discover the cause of his illness. After the results of an MRI of his lungs, the doctor asked him if he'd ever been exposed to asbestos. "Yes," he said, "but oh, my, that was seventy years ago." He told the doctor that when his family lived in Drummondville, Quebec, they traveled nearly every weekend to the nearby town of Asbestos (named after its valuable asbestos mines) to play soccer. The doctor told Dad that the MRI showed evidence of asbestos exposure, which could cause pulmonary fibrosis, and it didn't really matter how long ago it had been. His breathing difficulties would only worsen, the doctor said, and they would try to make him as comfortable as possible.

In his later years, I always looked forward to seeing Dad or even taking him to a doctor's appointment. It was nearly impossible to feel resentful toward him, no matter how much care he needed, since he never complained about anything and never failed to give a heartfelt thanks for all I and others did for him.

• • •

Dad's thoughts on World War II evolved over the years. My son, Ben, interviewed him for a high school class project in 1999, and Ben asked him why he'd volunteered to fight in the war. Dad said:

I felt that Hitler had to be stopped for the good of our country, for our freedom. He just kept getting stronger and stronger, and there was no telling how far he could go or what he would do. If he'd gotten the atom bomb, for instance, the consequences were too terrible to think about—and they were working on it, we now know.

When Ben asked him how he'd been affected by the war, he replied:

> It's hard to say—there's a certain satisfaction that you survived, of course. But there is also a grief and sadness that you think of. Even last night when I was thinking of what to say to you today, I started remembering people I'd been friends with in the war.
>
> So I was glad to do what I could, glad I made it through, but it also made me feel that I wouldn't be surprised if 100 years from now historians and other analysts will say that World War II, like the First World War, was a terrible, cruel waste, an infliction of suffering on millions and millions of people that never needed to happen. Winston Churchill was, of course, a brilliant, energetic genius. If he had devoted himself in the 1920s to helping solve the economic problems of Germany, and if we had done the same while Hitler was trying to get a foothold, it would have changed the entire picture. But we were shortsighted.

The tendency to romanticize World War II was distasteful to Dad. He would have agreed with Rick Atkinson, author of *An Army at Dawn: The War in North Africa, 1942–1943* and *The Day of Battle: The War in Sicily and Italy, 1943–1944* (two books in a trilogy on World War II), who said:

> You have to be wary of romanticized historical retrospection: 292,000 Americans died in WWII and 60 million people died worldwide. To wish that we were somehow back in WWII, or

to wish to be fighting in a war like that is to wish for awful things to befall the civilized world. If you go back and look at any publication from the corresponding time in 1944, you will see a nation totally and completely at war, from the advertisements to the book reviews. The leadership had convinced the country that it was fighting an existential war that required the commitment of the entire population. Even though we've been told that Iraq is an existential war, there's been no concomitant effort to involve the country. Soldiers know that. Soldiers feel that.[5]

The historical filmmaker Ken Burns, who produced the public television documentary miniseries *The War*, echoes Atkinson's sentiments: "The Second World War has often been smothered over in bloodless gallant death as the 'Good War,' but of course it was in reality the worst war."[6]

Dad went on to tell Ben in their interview:

If people had said, well, spend a hundred million and help them [the Germans] get straightened out, which we did eventually anyway, it would have saved a lot of trouble. Because that's where Hitler got his strength, from the unemployed, economic unrest, and general problems of the country. He took advantage of that. That's part of the legacy—if we'd started earlier, had a Marshall Plan then instead of later, 50 million people might not have died in the space of a few years . . . an awful cost of human suffering. If people had been wiser, more unselfish, more tolerant, and had a broader view of what was needed, it could have been done.

• • •

Dad weakened as the pulmonary fibrosis progressed. His vitality began to ebb. He'd always had a stiff-upper-lip attitude toward his health, pushing himself hard and never complaining, but even with the oxygen tank and a walker, his breath was so short he refused to go for walks outside. Still, when asked how he was doing, he always tried to sound upbeat. "Not quite as good as I'd like, but I hope to feel better soon."

I began to notice that when I told certain people that he had pulmonary fibrosis, their faces would fall. These were people who had personal experience with the disease and knew what the end would be like. As one physician described it, "It's like having someone hold your head underwater for three or four months, and then you die."

Now, instead of being out front as the "leader of the band," Dad watched from his chair as life's activities went on around him, orchestrated by others. But he continued to write for the newspaper and smiled when he saw his byline, especially when it appeared on the front page.

His hearing was failing but he balked at wearing his hearing aid, which he liked to say cost more than his first house. Thus, conversations would often be drowned out by the blaring TV—his favorite shows being *The NewsHour with Jim Lehrer*, live broadcasts of the meetings of the Fairfax County Board of Supervisors, and Baltimore Orioles baseball games.

Ruth phoned one August morning in 2004 to say that she'd called an ambulance to take Dad to the hospital—he was in distress and gasping for breath. She needed to go to work, and could I come be with him until the ambulance arrived? I drove across the Potomac River on Chain Bridge to McLean, as I'd done a thousand times before, but nervously this time. When I got to Dad's apartment, I found him sitting up in the bedroom, relieved to see me, even though Ruth had left only moments before. The ambulance soon arrived. The EMTs maneuvered the stretcher inside and placed him on it, making sure his oxygen was in place. As they wheeled him out of the apartment, he cautioned them not to hurt themselves going around the corner in the hallway, and he told them how much he appreciated their help. I fought back tears, touched by his graciousness. I wondered if he was thinking, as I was, that this might be the last time he'd see the home where he and Ruth had been so happy.

During the next few weeks, my sister Marty made frequent trips from Pennsylvania to see Dad in the hospital, and both my brothers came and went. On the highest level of oxygen now, Dad still couldn't get enough air since his air passages were shrinking with each day that passed and there was little room for the breath he tried so desperately to take in.

Ruth and her friend Jeanne traditionally headed to Boston every year at this time. I was glad when they decided to go. Of course, she'd hesitated to leave him but he seemed somewhat improved; he encouraged her, knowing she needed the rest and the diversion. Since she worked in the hospital where he was staying, she was frequently in his room. When Ruth was around, he wanted to be with her all the time, and she wanted to be with him. But this little girl wanted her daddy back, and now—with Ruth away—I finally had him to myself (except for doctors, nurses, and other visitors). I held his hand and brought him the newspaper. I moved closer to him, pulling my chair up right beside his bed or even sitting on the bed. But Ruth was uncomfortable being away from him, and after a day or two, she and Jeanne returned.

We knew it was time for a conversation with him about going into hospice. Ruth, Marty, and I had parsed out how much to tell Dad about his condition. Finally, one heartbreaking day, his doctor (an old friend of the family) sat down alone with Dad and told him he needed to prepare for death. Afterward, Dad and Ruth held hands and he said, "I thought we'd have more time."

On her birthday, August 25, she and I left him at the hospital in the evening. He had the TV remote in hand, waiting for his

beloved Orioles to begin play, and we went out for a birthday dinner at his favorite restaurant. That night, Ruth told me her father
had died on her mother's birthday some years before, and then we
talked a bit about what kind of funeral service Dad might want.

• • •

I'd always wanted to say "I love you" to his face. I wanted to
look right into his brown eyes and say it. I wanted to say it before we left the hospital that night, but I didn't.

It would be nice to say that my father and I finally had a moment of bonding, of saying all that wanted and needed to be
said, but that didn't happen.

He came down in the darkness like an oak, alone and quiet
as a whisper.

At one-thirty in the morning, I got the call that he'd died.
Ruth was sorry that he died alone, but he probably didn't want
to trouble anyone with it. And he'd waited until the early morning hours of August 26 so that he wouldn't die on her birthday.

The man who stood between me and mortality was gone at
age 86—the man who sung "Danny Boy" to me as a child, who
told me to save $5 a week (would that I had done it), who never
missed a birthday or an event of importance, who wrote his
parents every single Sunday they were alive, and who worried
about my mother long after she'd left him.

Many of his characteristics are scattered throughout the
makeup of his children: his love of writing, his deep feeling for
the underdog, his difficulty expressing emotion, and his dry wit.
The facts of an obituary or the sentiments of a eulogy don't
serve to describe him or what he meant to us. My world shrank
a little when he died.

I went downstairs that night to phone family members
about Dad's death. Ben, who was nineteen, heard us awake and

talking. He came down and stood on the stairway. Ben and his grandfather had a loving and respectful relationship and were devoted to each other. Ben wrote a long report about him in the tenth grade when he and his classmates were assigned to write about someone they admired. He was about to go back to college for his sophomore year and had just gone to see his grandfather in the hospital the day before. Now, he hugged me tight and then said in a soft voice, "I told him I loved him, Mom. And he said he loved me, too."

Somehow that smoothed out the ragged edges for me. Bless them both, I thought. That's plenty enough for me. Maybe the inability to say it skips a generation. I was proud of Ben, and felt such love for them both—my father and my son. The circle was complete.

NOTES

1. Mark Van Ells, *To Hear Only Thunder Again: America's World War II Veterans Come Home* (Lanham, Md.: Lexington Books, 2001), p. 116.

2. ————, "The Rough Road to Readjustment," *VFW Magazine*, December 2002.

3. Ibid.

4. Dr. Ursano is Professor of psychiatry and neuroscience at the Uniformed Services University of the Health Sciences in Bethesda, Maryland, and director of the Center for the Study of Traumatic Stress.

5. "Department of Advice: Greatest Generation Edition," *Washington Post*, Outlook Section, November 26, 2006.

6. "In His Own Words: Filmmaker Ken Burns on The War," *WETA Magazine*, September, 2007.

CHAPTER NINE

KZ-Ebensee

"Permit me to tell you what you would have seen and heard had you been with me on Thursday. It will not be pleasant listening."

—Edward R. Murrow, broadcasting live from Buchenwald, April 15, 1945

I stood on soggy ground over the makeshift graves of hundreds of concentration camp prisoners in Ebensee, Austria, on May 7, 2005, less than a year after my father's death. An icy rain fell from the dismal, gray sky, and the rising mist allowed only a partial view of the Alps. I was surrounded by some 2,000 people who had come to commemorate the sixtieth anniversary of the liberation of KZ-Ebensee (Konzentrationslager Ebensee) by the American Army and to honor those who had suffered so unspeakably and died here.

A subcamp of Mauthausen, Ebensee had provided slave labor for the construction of twenty-five tunnels on two levels dug into the mountainside in which to produce secret armaments for the Nazis. Deep in the hills near Lake Traunsee in Austria's Salzkammergut region, the camp facilities and structures had all but disappeared except for the main gate and the chimney of the crematorium.

Two years earlier, at the urging of my friend Ursula Junk—a journalist with a particular interest in the Holocaust—I'd asked my father about the camp he'd seen during the war. "Where was Ebensee?" I asked. "Was it a concentration camp?"

"Yes, it was a death camp just south of Gmunden, Austria," he replied.

Since I had first spoken with my father about Ebensee, I'd been learning all I could. I knew seeing the camp had made an indelible impression on him, but it was too difficult for him to talk about, and I wanted to find out more about it on my own. Ursula had told me about the commemoration in 2005 and had encouraged me to go. Only illness prevented her from leaving her home in Cologne to attend as well.

Instead, my friend Kathy Fitch joined me for the trip from her home in Madrid, Spain. It meant a lot to me to have her with me. She had known my family nearly her whole life since we'd been best friends since age 11. Two British friends came to meet us in Ebensee, Vivien Stern and Andrew Coyle. They knew I was writing about my father's war experiences, including the camp, and wanted to be there for the commemoration.

On the morning of May 7, we enjoyed a wonderful Austrian breakfast of birchermuesli cereal, hot coffee with lots of hot milk, dark bread dense with pumpkin seeds, and plum jam. As we set off in our rental car for the opening ceremonies, I was filled with both uneasiness and excitement about the day ahead. I wanted to learn more about the camp and its liberation, yet I dreaded the deep suffering we would hear about.

Because the road was unmarked, we had to ask for directions twice. I was afraid we'd get lost and miss the planned morning speeches, but soon, gathering crowds signaled the way. We approached rows of houses that had been built directly on top of the spot where the camp had stood. My discomfort level rose at the thought that someone could build and live in a house on land tainted with the blood of the approximately 8,300 people who had died at the camp and the suffering of so many more. This region of Austria reminded me of the children's book *Heidi*—snow-capped mountain peaks, valleys dotted with neat farmhouses, a healthy and well-scrubbed population. And yet a terrible past was buried here. I wondered what people in the town felt as visitors trooped in each year for the anniversary of the liberation of the camp: ashamed, detached, or appreciative for the tourist business?

We parked and walked down the dirt path past the houses. A young boy beckoned, selling or giving away tea and biscuits to the visitors, but we didn't stop. I paused as we passed the spot where the original entrance to the camp had been and imagined my father as a young soldier standing there entering the camp. What must have gone through his mind at KZ-Ebensee? Did he grasp what he was witnessing? I hoped to find some answers by talking to others who were there during those days marked by horror and hope.

On entering the memorial space, we noticed a sheltered area known as the "Italian wall." Over the years, people who had come from Italy had created a permanent collection of plaques with the names, photos, and dates of birth and death of loved ones who had perished in the camp. Flowers and candles adorned the wall.

The anniversary brought together survivors of the camp, U.S. soldiers who had liberated them, all their families, and others. A large group came from Italy. Groups from Poland, France, Russia, Greece, and Ukraine also gathered on the damp grounds to honor their dead and renew their common vow of "Never again."

One stage was set up for speakers, another for musicians. A group of Polish survivors of the camp, all wearing identical blue and white striped scarves and dressed in prison gray striped shirts and hats, prayed at a special Polish memorial. Some wore badges displaying the numbers tattooed on their arms, indicating that they had also been at Auschwitz.

After seating ourselves at the long benches in front of the stage, we awaited the speeches in the chilled, steady rain. The remains of the tall stone chimney of the crematorium stood to our left. The burgermeister (mayor) of the town of Ebensee opened the formalities around 11 A.M. by welcoming the visitors (some of whom didn't sit for the speeches, preferring to talk among themselves or go up to the tunnel). Former U.S. Army Sergeant Robert Persinger followed the mayor at the podium. Persinger wore a scarf matching those of the Polish survivors. Earlier that morning, one of the Poles, seeing that he was a liberator, had walked up to him and wordlessly placed the scarf around his neck.

Persinger represented F Company of the 3rd Cavalry Reconnaissance Squadron, part of the 3rd Cavalry Group (Mechanized) in which he had served during the war. In 1945, the job of the 3rd Cavalry Group—which was attached to the XX Corps of Patton's Third Army—was to scout for information for the 80th Infantry Division. Troops from the 3rd Cavalry Recon Squadron were the first U.S. Army units at Ebensee and the first to enter the camp, liberating its prisoners. Persinger told the crowd:

> It's hard for me to realize that nice homes have been built on these grounds, grounds that sixty years ago supported up to 18,000 prisoners, filthy barracks, and a crematorium with a barbed wire electrified fence around it. The sole entrance was through the archway that still stands today. The horrible sights we saw back then are stored in our memories, and those memories will never be erased.

One by one, survivors—all men over eighty years of age—
took the podium to speak of having worked eleven-hour days in
all types of weather with no break, and of the short life span of
workers attempting to survive on a starvation food allowance.
Two of the men said that if the soldiers had come even one day
later, they would have died. One said he was so hungry he
sometimes ate coal, grass, or clay. Andrew Sternberg left the
camp weighing only fifty-nine pounds. He had nowhere to go
when a local couple took him in. Their twenty-seven-year-old
son had been killed in the last days of the war and they wanted
to adopt Andrew Sternberg as their own. "It was at moments
like this that I sensed my life returning to me," said Sternberg.
"I was once again being seen and treated as a human being."

The town of Ebensee had not been eager to face up to its
past. Since much of the work carried out by the prisoners took
place in public, it was impossible for the people of the town not
to have realized what was taking place. But decades passed during which they refused to ask themselves what they could or
should have done. Only in the late 1980s did discussions take
place about building the museum and memorial—and both
were still controversial in 2005.

"The hills are alive with the sound of *murder*," cried Andrew
Sternberg from the podium, playing on the title of the musical
The Sound of Music, which was filmed nearby. Sternberg—who
was just a boy of fourteen when the Germans took him from
Hungary to a series of concentration camps, the last being
Ebensee—had come to the commemoration with his wife, son,
and grandchildren. "The hills are alive with the sound of *torture*," Sternberg thundered, his voice filled with anger and
grief. I felt a chill as I saw Julie Andrews in my mind's eye, dancing and twirling, singing the title song.

The speeches ended and liberators and survivors mingled,
often through their tears. A small group of us watched as

someone took a Polish survivor by the hand and led him over to Andrew Sternberg. They spoke no common language, but the man who introduced them spoke to each in his own language, telling them they'd both come from another camp, Melk, together to Ebensee. Sternberg and the Polish man smiled, looked into each other's eyes, and embraced. They kissed on both cheeks, then drew back to look at each other again, arms still clasped, eyes filling with tears. They embraced again and again and exchanged looks as if in disbelief and joy that they were alive today to see and touch each other.

Bob Persinger walked quietly through the crowd, giving out pins he had had made in the United States to bring to the survivors. I looked to see what the pins said: "Never again."

Emotions ran deep as the crowd continued to mix and make connections with the past—children and elders, people of many nationalities, old survivors and old American soldiers. A man who had survived the camp approached one of the American liberators and thanked him for saving his life. The former soldier wept as he clasped hands with the man. The survivor presented his wife and children to the soldier as if to say, "We wouldn't be here had you not come when you did." Words were spoken that neither understood, but their meaning was fully appreciated.

I struck up a conversation with Andrew Sternberg's son, Sandy. As we walked up to the tunnel that now housed a museum, Sandy introduced me to Andrew and the rest of the family. He said his father had talked often about the camp, and I told him that my father, the soldier, had never spoken of it. We exchanged a look that acknowledged how differently the two fathers dealt with their memories.

The tunnel was freezing and damp, even in May. It was impossible to imagine the thinly clad and often shoeless prisoners working outdoors all winter long on starvation rations. I looked on as Andrew Sternberg gently guided his young grandson through the exhibits. Now and then he would lean over and speak to him softly. Stopping in front of a photo taken of a group of emaciated survivors just after the liberation, the boy looked up and asked, "Are you in that picture, Grandpa?" Sternberg shook his head and said, "I don't know. I can't recognize myself."

My friends Kathy, Andrew, and Vivien had come up to the tunnel earlier and were looking at the photos and accompanying text (in both English and German). We maneuvered our way down the slippery path back to the cemetery grounds.

• • •

When it was built in 1943, Ebensee was intended as a slave labor camp, not an "extermination" or "death" camp. The tunnel system was originally designed to replace the Nazis' missile testing station at Peenemunde, Germany, which had been partially destroyed by British bombs. The station manufactured V-weapons, small pilotless aircraft that caused great apprehension among English and Belgian civilians. In response to the bombings of Peenemunde, Albert Speer (the Nazi minister for armaments and war production), Heinrich Himmler (the head of the SS), and Adolf Hitler opted to build a new facility deep in the mountains in Austria. Surrounded by mountains and tall fir trees, Ebensee was thought to be an ideal location in case of attack by Allied ground troops. It also had ready-made access to railway lines.

But before long, plans for missile production were abandoned. Allied bombing of German fuel production facilities and armament plants required the building of new ones. One of the tunnels to be built at Ebensee was slated for petroleum refining; others would be outfitted with machinery to produce engine components for tanks and trucks. The armament industry wanted to use alien civilians, prisoners of war, and concentration camp inmates as laborers, so the SS hired the inmates out to the building contractors commissioned to construct the tunnels. To maximize the performance of the undernourished prisoners, the SS subjected them to systematic terror, even setting up a special SS tunnel police unit to beat them with ox-whips and clubs.

Ebensee served a different purpose from that of Auschwitz and other camps. The official "extermination" camps were all in Poland—Auschwitz-Birkenau, Belzec, Treblinka, Majdanek, Chelmno, and Sobibor—and were designed to process and kill large numbers of Jews and Roma (also Gypsies). Although the other concentration camps, such as Ebensee, were also places of wretchedness and death, the authorities in those camps killed the prisoners by attrition as well as by order of the commandants. After the prisoners were worked to death, starved to death, or a combination of the two, they would be replaced by others. In fact, the SS assumed large numbers of prisoners would die in the digging, and so they constructed a crematorium in the spring of 1944 to burn the bodies of those who had died.

More than 27,000 people were imprisoned at Ebensee between the opening of the camp and its liberation. They came from Belgium, the Netherlands, Luxembourg, France, Denmark, and Norway as well as Poland, the Baltic States, Hungary, Romania, and Czechoslovakia. The camp housed Jews, Roma, and Sinti (also Gypsies) as well as prisoners of war, homosexuals, political prisoners, and members of the intelligentsia—anyone deemed racially inferior or a potential troublemaker.

As in all of their camps, the Nazis created a class system among the prisoners to keep them from organizing and developing any sense of solidarity. At the top of the heap were Germans considered "political" and "criminal" opponents of the Nazi Party, followed by prisoners from western or southern Europe. Citizens of the Soviet Union and Poland ranked lower in the racist hierarchy. At the very bottom of the scale were Jews and Roma or Sinti of any nationality.

"It was obvious that they [Jews] were singled out for particularly bad treatment. They had to work day and night shifts," said one former inmate. "Their working hours were particularly long . . . all Jews had to carry out their work at a running pace."

Inmates were forced into unspeakably hard labor. "Kapos," often German convicts, were selected by the SS to supervise the inmates' work while not being required to work themselves. Their primary task was to "encourage" the prisoners with ox-whips, rubber batons, sticks, knotted ropes, and iron rods. Apart from the exhausting daily labor, the prisoners were forced to stand on the Roll Call Square for hours on end and to endure torture by Kapos. Escape was impossible: The camp was surrounded by an electrified barbed wire fence and towers manned by armed guards.

Prisoners arose at 4:30 A.M. for half a liter of watery coffee, then fell out for roll call and left for work assignments at 6 A.M. At noon, they received three-quarters of a liter of hot water with a spoonful of potato peelings, which were often rotten. The evening meal consisted of half a liter of "bread" made from morsels of coal, stone, and unidentifiable materials, and watery tea.

Weakness was punished. Of the sick or injured prisoners, only those expected to recover received medical attention. The rest were left to die or were exterminated. In the barracks, the stronger inmates would often procure the top bunks. Weaker inmates could not climb up and so were left on the bottom where the sawdust fell on them from the mattress above. Three men frequently shared one wooden bunk.

Georg Bachmayer served as the camp's first commandant. Bachmayer liked to tie a prisoner's arms behind him, hands side-by-side and thumb-to-thumb, and suspend him from a tree about eighteen inches off the ground. He then let loose his German shepherd, "Lord," on the prisoner, who died a slow and agonizing death.

The camp's second commandant was Otto Reimer. Conditions deteriorated even further under his rule as he shot, tortured, and beat prisoners daily, offering extra cigarettes and leave time to guards who caused the largest numbers of deaths. One trick the guards used to raise the count was to knock the cap off a prisoner and throw it into the forbidden area between the barracks and the electrified fence. When the prisoner went to retrieve it, he was shot and killed.

Anton Ganz commanded the camp in its last year, from May 1944 through early May 1945. "During the day Ganz spends his time hunting down men who are not working," said former inmate Jean Lafitte in 1950, as recounted in the Ebensee museum brochure. "Ganz is everywhere. He turns up unexpectedly with his riding whip and hits people in the face wildly. Sometimes he just pulls out his revolver and kills someone."[1]

Surviving inmates recalled that "hunger turned us into walking skeletons who either showed no reactions at all or behaved like wild animals. Individual prisoners or groups of prisoners attacked each other for a few crumbs of bread."[2] The final death toll for Ebensee reached more than 8,300 people, out of the 27,000 total imprisoned there.

• • •

As the war began to wind down and the Russians began their advance into Poland, the Germans were forced to evacuate the

Polish camps. Mass evacuations from these camps put tremendous pressure on Mauthausen, which was the last remaining complex under German control, as prisoners (mainly Jews) were dispersed by cattle train to Mauthausen and its subcamps in Austria—among them Melk, Gusen, and Ebensee. The twenty-five barracks at Ebensee, designed to hold 100 prisoners each, sometimes held 750 at this point. To this number were added the prisoners being kept in the tunnel systems and outside under the open sky. The naked bodies of the deceased lay stacked up outside the crematorium, which was unable to keep pace. Commandant Ganz ordered that the corpses be thrown into mass graves. In the closing weeks of the war, the death rate exceeded 350 a day.

For those who managed to survive in the camps, confusion in the Nazi political realm coupled with the overcrowding caused even further deterioration of already unbearable living conditions. The camps became even worse breeding grounds for diseases such as typhus, dysentery, and tuberculosis among dehydrated and starving inmates. At this point, food rations at Ebensee were stretched to almost nothing, and even the guards fought over that which was available. When all these factors were added to the enormous strain of the workload, the numbers of casualties and deaths drastically increased. As the piles of the dead grew larger by the day, nervous camp authorities began to look for ways to dispose of prisoners, thus covering up their despicable acts.

Nearly 2,000 inmates had arrived at Ebensee from Auschwitz on January 29, 1945. The trip lasted eleven days in open cattle cars, with no food, drink, or toilet facilities. Ebensee survivor Herman Roth remembers that civilians threw food, such as sandwiches, into the open railroad cars for the prisoners, but such intense fighting ensued over the items that few benefited from

them. So many died in transit to Ebensee that the inmates used
the stiff, dead bodies as benches to sit on. Roth and his father
had managed to stay together, surviving Auschwitz and the trip
to Ebensee, only to have Roth's father die one week prior to
liberation.

The journeys ending at Ebensee had all begun years earlier,
however: The German invasion of Poland, the ghettoization of
the Jews in Warsaw and other cities, *Kristallnacht* (the pogrom
throughout Germany that destroyed thousands of Jewish businesses, homes, and synagogues in November 1938 and became
the prelude to the annihilation of millions of Jews), and many
other events led up to the scenes witnessed by the Allied soldiers at liberation.

Max Garcia, one of the survivors of Ebensee, was a Dutch
Sephardic Jew. He had lived in Amsterdam with his parents and
sister, Sienie. One night in early December 1942, sixteen-year-
old Sienie was picked up in a street raid by the Nazis, even
though her work permit was in order. In one of our interviews,
Garcia said:

> We never saw her again. When my mother realized Sienie was
> gone, she screamed and tried to throw herself out the window.
> I found out after the war my sister been gassed at Auschwitz,
> but at the time we knew nothing about concentration camps
> or gas chambers. My parents sent me into hiding but after
> several moves I was betrayed and discovered. Just before that I
> saw my parents for the last time on my nineteenth birthday. In
> order to visit me secretly, they had to remove the yellow stars
> on their outer garments [Jews in the Netherlands were
> required to wear a Star of David to identify themselves] and
> leave their papers behind, which was very dangerous. Some
> months later they were also picked up and taken to Sobibor, in
> eastern Poland, where they were gassed on my mother's
> birthday, July 16, 1943.

Garcia was herded into a sealed boxcar and shipped to Auschwitz. Over the course of the next years, he survived pneumonia, acute appendicitis, and an abscessed finger. In January 1945, he was shipped by open railroad car to Mauthausen under such frigid conditions that many died en route. From there, he was transferred to the subcamp at Melk, and then finally on to Ebensee in April, where he was put to work in the icy tunnels. He eked out an existence until liberation on May 6. Despite the short duration of his stay at Ebensee, Garcia says that the camp is very important to him because it is the camp he was liberated from and the camp he would have died in.

Of those last days there, he says, "There was no food anymore—that was really the bad part. And the sleeping, you slept three to four to a bunk. So we knew the end was in sight, we just didn't know if we would live that long." Garcia said that on May 4, 1945:

> We were called out to Roll Call Square on Friday morning [some accounts say this took place on Saturday, May 5]. The SS guards were all around with their guns trained on us. Then something happened that had never happened before: Ganz himself appeared and addressed us as "gentlemen." Because the Allies were approaching, he told us we should go into the tunnels to avoid being caught in the crossfire between the Allies and the SS. He said he knew the SS would fight until the last man, and he wanted to protect us. When he finished talking in German and it was translated, people started saying *NO! nyet! nein! non!*—in all languages, louder and louder. Ganz and his officers were taken aback by the defiance. The SS withdrew and we didn't go to work that day.

With that incident, more than 16,000 men who had been living as subhumans regained a bit of their dignity. The prisoners recognized the ploy for what it was: a wanton attempt to eliminate all witnesses to the horrors of Ebensee by blowing up the tunnels and thus silencing them once and for all. Garcia continued:

> When we woke up Saturday morning, the SS had gone. First thing, we cut off the electricity so the wires were not dangerous. The Russian prisoners climbed the wire and got into the kitchen. They were eating food like crazy, no regard. We didn't care at that juncture. One of the Kapos was shoved into the crematorium and burned alive.

• • •

Meanwhile, the U.S. troops were approaching. While the anti-Semitic nature of the Nazi regime was well known. American troops were too preoccupied with their own piece of the war to give much thought to the concentration camps. Many had heard of them but believed them to be more like the German POW camps they'd encountered, which were unhealthy and punitive but not the unimaginable horrors the soldiers later saw at places like Ebensee and Buchenwald.

On Sunday, May 6, formal surrender of the German Army was in sight but still two days away when A Troop of the 3rd Cavalry Recon Squadron, traveling with F Company of the same squadron, arrived in the town of Ebensee. They heard from the townspeople that a concentration camp lay at the foot of the mountains just outside town, and two jeeps from A Troop were sent to investigate. Meanwhile, B Troop was rolling into the nearby town of Traunkirchen. A small unit from B Troop was promptly dispatched to the camp by a different route, and the two units never crossed paths. The A Troop soldiers returned almost immediately to the town of Ebensee, while B Troop drove the few miles back to Traunkirchen after communicating the exact coordinates of the camp to 3rd Squadron

Headquarters. Upon receiving news of the concentration camp, Lieutenant Colonel Marshall Wallach, the squadron commander, directed F Company, a tank outfit, to send two tanks and a jeep to take a closer look and see what was needed.

At 2:50 P.M., tank crews led by Sergeants Robert Persinger and Dick Pomante reached the gates of the camp. The soldiers' jaws dropped at the sight of ghost-like human beings dressed in filthy striped clothes that barely covered their bodies. The prisoners were skin and bones; it was evident they were starving.

Persinger's tank arrived first. Furious at what he saw, he reached out and grabbed the rifle out of the hands of one of the *Volkssturm*, the elderly German soldiers who'd been left behind by the SS to guard the camp. He broke it in two over his gun turret and hung it over the light that illuminated the entranceway.

Persinger and Pomante drove through the gate, which had been opened from the inside by the prisoners. Their tanks rolled into the middle of the roll call area, where they stopped to observe and to decide what to do with the mass of prisoners surrounding them. No operating procedure existed for dealing with this situation. Never having seen human beings in this condition, they hesitated to make contact, tossing out energy bars and rations from the safety of the tanks.

The scene was chaotic with tumultuous cheers, embraces, and tears on the part of the dazed and deliriously happy prisoners. The appearance of the American Army meant freedom from their torture and suffering. Though they were covered with lice and open sores, they wanted to touch the soldiers to make sure they were real, to thank them, and they began to swarm the tanks. The soldiers were overwhelmed by their need, their near-death condition, and their smell. "I'll never forget the tank that came in and broke the gate of the camp," said survivor Morris Rubell.

I'll never forget their faces. They looked happy, haggard, dusty, full of love and caring, throwing candy, giving things to us. And yet they were bewildered. They never saw anything like this before. They were shocked. They wanted to help but they couldn't. We wanted to see happiness and maybe we saw what we wanted to see. But they saw death all around them.

"I lit a cigarette," said Sergeant Persinger, "and heard someone say, 'It's been a long time since I smoked a Lucky Strike.' I asked him to climb up on the tank so I could give him one." That's how the 3rd Cavalry met Max Garcia. At the time, Garcia was twenty years old and weighed approximately eighty-five pounds.

Garcia pressed the soldiers to look around the camp area, but at first they refused. Persinger, reluctant to dismount, knew they would have to wade through the teeming sea of bodies as well as the quagmire of mud and corpses with its unbearable stench. But Garcia convinced them they needed to see more. Only by going inside the camp could one comprehend the human degradation. Being good soldiers, they put boots to the ground and entered the compound.

They visited the crematorium. Bodies stacked like cordwood one on top of the other lay around the sides of the building. Some parts of the piles still moved. The people were not just naked; they'd been stripped of their hair and the gold in their teeth.

Then the soldiers came upon bodies with their heads and arms cut off. "What's this?" they asked Garcia. "Revenge," he said—fellow prisoners who'd behaved brutally and were murdered by others who finally had the upper hand, since they didn't have to fear the SS anymore. The soldiers struggled to keep their composure. "I've been in battle, seen a lot of combat, a lot of dead people, but never this—arms and heads cut off, people being quartered. It's beyond imagination," Persinger later said.

The next urgent task was to find food for the 16,000 starving prisoners. The cavalry platoon, with Garcia in tow as their translator, returned to the Post Hotel in the village to arrange for food and much needed medical care. When Captain Timothy Brennan sent word to all infantry units nearby to fan out and bring food to the camp, trucks began to arrive with potatoes, cabbage, and other vegetables collected from miles around.

In the meantime, those boots Persinger had put on the ground at Ebensee smelled so terrible that he burned them. Sergeant Pomante, who was driving his tank down the main street of town, made a stop in front of the bakery and ordered the owner to turn over all his goods for the camp. When he refused, Pomante thought perhaps he didn't understand, and he repeated his order. This time he knew he'd been understood, but the baker still balked at the idea of providing free bread for the prisoners. Pomante steered his tank right up to the front window of the bakery and threatened to blast the store off the map, thus persuading the baker to donate the bread.

Back at the camp, the soldiers prepared soup but soon realized that somehow they had to control the distribution. Crazed with hunger, inmates stormed the soup lines and GIs had to resort to firing live ammunition over their heads. This brought the situation under control, but many gulped down the hot, rich soup so fast that they died as a result of intestinal disorders.

Max Garcia became an unofficial member of F Company because of his usefulness as a translator. Captain Brennan got him the smallest uniform he could find. "You could see every bone in my body," Garcia recalled.

"Every time I recall having yelled, 'It's been a long time since I had a Lucky Strike,' to a liberating American tank crewman," said Garcia, "I thank my father for teaching me to think on my feet and for insisting I learn some English. That yelled phrase changed the course of my life."

After General Eisenhower saw the concentration camp at Ohrdruf, Germany, a satellite camp of Buchenwald, he issued immediate orders to local people who lived near any U.S.-liberated camp to go inside to witness the suffering. He was infuriated at the way people outside the camps insisted they had not known what took place. As the German civilians filed by the stacks of corpses in the camps, some fainted.

Captain Brennan also instructed the citizens of Ebensee during that first week to walk through the camp and see it for themselves. In fact, he required the women to clean the barracks and the men to place the corpses on wagons and move them to mass graves along the Ischler Strasse that ran by the Traun River between Ebensee and the town of Bad Ischl. A continuous cemetery would forever remind the citizens of Ebensee and nearby towns of the shame of the camp that had blighted their town. Prisoners did tell the soldiers, however, that some townspeople had smuggled them food, water, and cigarettes at the risk of imprisonment, or even their lives.

• • •

During this time, my father was with E Company nearby, probably in Gmunden, a town at the top of Lake Traun. He assisted in gathering up the German Sixth Army, which was surrendering by the thousands. Although hundreds of soldiers entered the camp at Ebensee during those days, some to observe and some to guard and care for the inmates, Dad went to the camp alone. He stood under the archway entrance where Persinger had hung the *Volkssturm* rifle and walked in. He was besieged by the prisoners with both vacant and happy looks, wanting to talk, needing food, and just wishing to express their thanks.

What he observed made a deep impression on him and affected him profoundly for the rest of his life. He would never be able to convey to his family the sights and smells he found impossible to comprehend at the time. Robert H. Abzug, author of *Inside the Vicious Heart: Americans and the Liberation of Nazi Concentration Camps*, writes, "The gulf of experience and expectation that lay between liberator and survivor, the different world that made battle-weary American innocents by comparison, disoriented and disturbed even those most ready to embrace the victims of Nazi terror."

The 515th Hospital Clearance Company had arrived the Tuesday after liberation and was soon followed by the 139th Evacuation Hospital. Lieutenant Jeannie Davis arrived in the town of Ebensee, serving as a nurse with the 139th. Her job, along with the doctors and medical technicians, was to get the inmates ready to evacuate to a regular hospital. The men went up to the camp first but a full week passed before they allowed the nurses to go. When I interviewed Davis, she told me:

> When we did go to the camp, and when I think of this, it was so idiotic—we took tablecloths up there. We thought we would try to make it pleasant for them. They had old wooden tables and they were bringing up better food for them. Of course, they were starving to death. They were in bunks, and many of them were still lying there, many of them dead. Every five minutes somebody would die, even weeks after liberation. It was so awful and there we were, these silly little nurses, putting tablecloths around.
>
> But it didn't shock us as much as others who were not nurses. Through our training, we'd seen everything. The fact that it was done deliberately, in such mass, was what made it different. But we were able to talk to them and stand next to the bunks. I can think of women I know who couldn't possibly have done that, but we could. We stayed for the day. And one day was enough, believe me. For someone like me it was like a

terrible, bad dream. How could people mistreat each other this way?

We helped them get their lunch. And of course they had not seen young women in so long, they just stared at us the whole time. But they had no emotion.

I couldn't possibly believe in any God after seeing that. I am an atheist. So in that way it affected my life.

Davis never talked to her children and grandchildren about what she had seen and experienced.

• • •

In 1948, the Ebensee municipal council decided to construct apartments on the former camp site. The KZ-Verband, a federal association of resistance fighters and former concentration camp inmates, managed to preserve the archway that had formed the entrance to the camp. Hilda Lepetit, the widow of one of Ebensee's victims, organized the placement of a memorial near the mass gravesite at the former crematorium in 1948. In 1953, the camp cemetery was relocated from Ischler Strasse to the Lepitit memorial. The memorial that carried the inscription "For the eternal disgrace of the German people" was blown up one year later so as not to inhibit tourism.

The last night of the Ebensee ceremonies in 2005, Kathy, Vivien, Andrew, and I went to a restaurant located back in the mountains. We walked into a small room that was like a beer hall, filled with booths, wooden tables, and locals. As we greeted the friendly owner, we noticed that all the men were at one table on one side of the room drinking beer, while the women were on the other side. Some of the men still wore their Tyrolean hats. As usual, Vivien translated the menu for us. I ordered Hungarian goulash, salad, and a beer. It sounded good on a cold, damp night.

As we waited for our dinner to arrive, we speculated on the men we saw—some looked of an age to have been involved at the camp. We dubbed one large man with cold blue eyes "The Guard."

We struggled to find the words to give expression to what we had seen, heard, and felt over the last two days. The word "liberation" had been used many times, yet it brought to mind a festive event, whereas the liberation at Ebensee evoked relief and empathy, as well as anger, horror, and despair at the 3rd Cavalry Recon's discovery. "Liberation" also meant an awful freedom because many survivors had no home to return to. Entire Jewish families had been killed and their homes destroyed; for them, liberation came too late. Many camp inmates were the only surviving members of their families. They were alive but without a life to return to. No one waited for them.

We talked about the word "liberator" and how all of the soldiers used it with humility, some even rejecting it as a name for themselves. They preferred to call themselves "witnesses."

When we learned about the Holocaust, we had all grown up with statistics and wrenching photographs, but over the last several days we had met real human beings who had been part of this ugly history. Each one had gone on to live a life and share a common purpose: to bear witness. As we sat at the wooden table in the restaurant in Ebensee, we were honored and moved to have been a part of it, to have seen the courage and humanity that arose out of the ashes of such abomination.

• • •

When Ursula had visited Al and me the previous year in June 2004, she asked to interview my father about his war experiences. Her special interest in concentration camps had been the moving force behind my investigation into the meaning of the box from Braunau. Dad agreed to talk with her. Since he had become weaker by this time and needed oxygen more often, we went to his apartment for the interview. Although he didn't want to talk about Ebensee, he agreed to because it was important to record what he saw of the Holocaust. But I knew he was also doing it for me.

Since it was Saturday, Ruth was there as well. Ursula greeted them both, set up her tape recorder, and pulled up a chair near Dad in the living room as Ruth and I sat on the couch off to the side. Ursula began to ask Dad questions, and before long, I was on the edge of the couch, feeling uncomfortable. Ursula spoke excellent English with a German accent. She was a warm and kind person, but her manner seemed brusque in contrast to Dad's. With his age and poor health, I worried the interview might be too demanding. Ursula wouldn't hesitate to question or contradict him if she felt the need. For his part, a lack of directness and his use of Army terminology only muddled the conversation.

It didn't start off well. Ursula knew Dad had been in Germany and Austria during the war, but things got garbled soon after the interview began. He told her about being in France when "General Patton ran out of gas," and he was about to tell her about being wounded in Rouves on November 8, 1944. He tried to tell her that Patton sent them into battle despite the bad weather.

Dad began, "And then on November the 8th, 1944, Patton said 'go.' There'd been three days of rain so we didn't think there was going to be any 'go' and everybody was relaxed, and then Patton said, 'Today, rain or no rain. Go.' "

Ursula asked if "go" meant going south in the direction of Austria.

He said no, to Germany. They were still in France, between Nancy and Metz, but headed for Germany. After that he'd gone from there to Nancy to Paris to Southampton to Liverpool and . . .

She interrupted him, "You went back to England?"

He nodded, but failed to explain that he'd gone to Paris, Southampton, and Liverpool from France because he'd been wounded and sent to England to recuperate.

"But when did you get to Austria?" Ursula asked.

In a careful, matter-of-fact tone, he said, "May of 1945."

She was already lost. "You did not get to Austria before that? What about Germany? You didn't spend any time in Germany?"

He shrugged. "Well, I spent some time there."

Then she asked if he'd been flown to Austria. He explained patiently that the Infantry didn't fly, they walked, crossing into Austria at Braunau. Ursula knew the box had come from there.

"What happened in Braunau?" she wanted to know.

There was little movement in the room. Ruth and I sat on the couch, listening. Dad sat in his chair very still, now and then moving his hand to scratch his nose or run his fingers through his hair.

"Well, there was no fighting there. We just moved in and there were a lot of prisoners."

"What kinds of prisoners?" she quizzed.

Ursula had assumed the box was given to Dad by a German, and Dad didn't correct her at first. My shoulders and neck tensed up. Dad seemed confused and I was nervous about what she'd say next. Dad's penchant for talking indirectly around a difficult subject wasn't helping or meshing well with Ursula's clipped and to-the-point questions.

She asked him if in Braunau "you actually ran into this German who gave you the box?"

"I have very little recollection.," he answered. "But he was quite young, quite literate, and friendly. And the box was about like so," showing the size of the box to be about eight inches by twelve inches, "silver color, and he'd made these different sketches of his hometown."

Ursula wanted to know why the man had given Dad the box.

"Well, he liked me," Dad replied. "We had quite a good conversation."

Ursula leaned forward and asked, "What did you talk about?"

He looked down at his hands, and replied, "Oh my, just where he'd been and how glad he was to see us. That sort of thing."

"Do you know where he was trying to get to? He wanted to stay in Braunau?"

"No, he wanted to go home to France."

"So he was a French prisoner?"

"Yes." You could hear his fatigue.

They went back and forth about whether the Russians or the Germans held French prisoners and where. "Are you sure," Ursula asked, "because the Russians had no French prisoners."

Silence. Dad shifted in his chair. His voice a little more firm, he said, "Well, he certainly had been a prisoner of the Russians, somewhere in there."

Ursula looked down at her notes as if deciding whether to pursue it further. "That may be," she said. Then, dropping that particular line of questioning, she asked, "So what was your first impression of the camp at Ebensee? What did you first see?"

"Civilians leaving the camp looking distressed," he responded.

They'd been forced to go through the camp. And then we saw these sort of boxcars the prisoners lived in. I remember that they were so pleased, so relieved, so overjoyed, to see us. But they couldn't say anything. Just "thank you" and we said we were glad to be there and we talked to them as much as we could but we could communicate very little. They were so hungry. We tried to give them food. And then they were told to stay within a certain area.

It was ironic—my father being quizzed by a German woman about a concentration camp—a German woman who was passionate about human rights and the suffering that Jews and others had endured. In the late 1960s, she'd gone to Mississippi to work during the civil rights struggles. Her entire life now was devoted to creating documentaries that would inform and educate people about civil and human rights.

"We tried to talk to them, but it was useless," Dad continued. "The language barrier was so bad and so many of them were too weak to talk anyhow. They showed us the furnace buildings."

"The crematorium, you mean."

Dad looked out the window to the courtyard and paused. "Yes. We just saw that from the outside. The stacks of bodies. It got to the point that it was just overwhelming and there wasn't anything you could do. We had soldiers there who were trying to help every way they could."

"So what was your function?"

"My function was just to observe. They said . . ." his voice trailed off.

"You did not have a particular duty there. You did not have to collect food. Just to see."

"No, we were stationed nearby and somebody said, 'If anybody wants to see the camp, now is the time.' So I went. I went by myself. Nobody with me."

She asked him why he decided to go and some others chose not to.

He sighed before answering. "I just had an interest in everything that was going on, and I wanted to see. When I did get to see it, I didn't know why I'd come. I was sorry I had. It was so devastating, so depressing. Frightening, really. So I just turned around and walked back." (I recalled Dad once telling me in a written note that he'd run into the woods afterward and he "couldn't see"—his code for "I was crying.")

Ursula's voice slowed. "Even after you'd spent that many months already in the war, it was horrible. More horrible than you could have imagined."

"It was worse, in a way, than combat," Dad replied. "I saw wounded in combat, of course, who were in terrible shape, but this was really bad. Well, the smell of it was so . . . overpowering. You could hardly stand it."

She asked if he'd spoken with any of the other soldiers about the experience, and he said yes. Some of them gave him pictures, which he said disappeared over the years. He then moved away from that subject and talked about how he and the other men were concerned about the Germans going into the "Redoubt" (a region in southern Austria), and that while they were interested in the prisoners, their main concern was to end the war.

"But to go back to the box," Ursula interjected, "since it all started with the box." She wanted to know why he'd kept it all these years.

"For heaven's sake," he said. "Well, it had pictures drawn on it. It was very unusual, no other box like it in the world. And also he was so friendly, so happy that we had come. I didn't ever expect him to give it to me. I was amazed when he said, 'Take it.' "

"You never tried to find out what happened to this man who gave you the box? And you're sure he was French?"

"We were able to talk, and I did speak some French, so I think so."

All of this questioning was hard on Dad, who was always happier in the role of the "questioner" than of the "questioned." But now that he was old and almost out of both breath and time, he was hesitant as he tried to remember things that had happened sixty years earlier. He was such a stickler for facts, I knew it bothered him when he didn't remember things. At the same time, I silently thanked Ursula for doing such an excellent job. She was doing exactly what she should have done—being persistent in a way I didn't have the heart to. I knew that if I'd been the one sitting by his side, seeing his weakened body as he struggled with his painful memories, I would have stopped after a few questions.

"But that he was French, you are sure?" she continued.

"I remember he was quite European. He came around, wanted to be friends with us. Showed me the box. Told me he'd been a prisoner of the Russians."

She gave up on the nationality of those who had held the man prisoner. She continued: "After the war, years after the war, you never tried to meet some of the other people from your unit and talk about that time?"

"No, I never did."

"Why not?"

"Well, some of them were dead, some of them were wounded. They all wanted to forget the whole thing. Nobody really wanted to talk about it except maybe the guys who were on the fringe. Ones who were in it where people were being shot up . . . there's no pleasure in talking about all that."

"But," she ventured, "it gives you some relief to talk about it."

"Maybe so, but I never felt it. None of the other guys did either."

"What about with your children? Why did you not talk about it with your children?"

"Well, it's an unpleasant subject, always, for me," he said in a voice that was so low it was almost inaudible. "I didn't want to talk about it. I did write a story of the war, which I can't find right now. Somewhere around here." He was referring to his combat journal. He looked like he'd like to get up and search for it.

"For whom did you write it?"

"For me. In the summer of 1945, in Germany. I sat down and wrote about it. Then I lost it, then I found it, then I lost it, found it, and now I've lost it again. But that's as much as I ever wanted to say. A lot of what people say about the war is not the full story, because it's so bad that they don't want to talk about it."

He shifted again, then looked up at her. He returned to the subject of the Russians, trying again to change the course of the conversation. She wouldn't let him, interrupting his story to ask him once more why he never spoke of it. He fiddled with a piece of paper, turned his head away from her, and replied in a soft voice, yet punctuating each word, "Well, it was just . . . *too awful.*"

NOTES

1. Jean Lafitte, from May 1945 interview, *Ebensee Concentration Camp*, 1997, (museum brochure).

2. Drahomir Barta and Vinco Bernot, May 1945, *Ebensee Concentration Camp*, 1997, (museum brochure).

CHAPTER TEN

Old Soldiers and Reunions

"We few, we happy few, we band of brothers;
For he today that sheds his blood with me
Shall be my brother."
—William Shakespeare, *Henry V*

On August 25, 2005—one year after my father's death—I packed up my tape recorder, camera, and computer and boarded an airplane for Columbus, Ohio, where the 80th Infantry Division was holding its annual reunion. I walked into the hotel and saw groups of old veterans and their wives scattered throughout the lobby and quietly talking. Some were in wheelchairs, while others were hooked up to oxygen tanks. Most wore baseball caps emblazoned with the slogan "The 80th Only Moves Forward." Some of the men were having a drink at the bar. A few looked hale and hearty. Each wore a badge bearing his name, the regiment, and the company with which he'd served.

My purpose in going to the reunion (which I now attend every year) was to add to my research. By that time, I'd spent many hours at the United States Holocaust Memorial Museum, the Witness to the Holocaust Project at Emory University, the National Archives, the Army Heritage and Education Center, and the Library of Congress. I enjoyed burrowing down in the library cubicles and leafing through old documents. But at this gathering, after just a few hours, I felt lost. I knew no one, and many of the attendees' friendships went back more than sixty years. Feeling a little sorry for myself, I wondered what I could gain from spending time with a group of World War II veterans who might not have even known my father.

I missed Dad more than usual and wished he could have shared in the society of this fraternity of men. I couldn't ask him why he never attended a reunion, but I imagined he didn't want to stir up the memories. Perhaps it would have been healing for him, as Ursula Junk had suggested, but I suspected he was afraid to release those long sealed-off emotions. And yet, he'd been interested in what his buddies were up to. He paid his annual dues to the 80th Division Veterans Association, and when he received the newsletter, *The Blue Ridge*, he made notes inside and underlined parts of articles he would send on to his children. He never defined himself by his military experience, but he was proud of it. Although the experiences of 80th Division soldiers were varied, the unifying factor for the men was that they all had risked their lives. Their memory banks contained shared sights and sounds, from the foreign names of the small European towns, to the awful "screaming meemies" as they zeroed in on a nearby foxhole, to the sight of shattered bodies.

But Dad wasn't here, and I wanted to continue my search with the soldiers who were here. After getting settled in my room, I went downstairs to pick up a registration packet. I looked on the bulletin board in the lobby for men who had served in Dad's unit, hoping to find someone who'd known him, but survivors of E Company were few.

The schedule for the gathering was full, consisting of banquets, dancing, speeches, administrative meetings, a tour of a nearby military museum, prayers, presentation of colors by the

color guard, and the playing of Taps. On the first full day, the attendees carried out one of the annual rituals: a memorial service
for those who had died during the previous year. Each man's
name was read along with his company, but rank was omitted so
that every person's life and death carried the same weight regardless of status in the Army. I wasn't sure whether Dad's name
would be read, since he'd died exactly a year earlier, but I was hit
with a disappointment that felt almost physical when I didn't
hear his name.

In between events, old friends hung around together. They
socialized, reminisced, compared health problems, refought the
war, and caught up on each other's lives. But most of all, they
came to say "We honor you and we will never forget you" to
those who died in battle, and to those who'd passed before
them. Each year, the old veterans come to the reunions, sometimes chauffeured by a wife, son, daughter, or grandchild. I
sensed they felt duty-bound to pay their respects to those who
didn't survive. It struck me how ingrained this notion of duty is
in the World War II generation, but they don't romanticize this
war, or any war. They lived through it.

I decided to interview other veterans of the 80th Division to
get some perspectives that were different from those of my father.
This was a way to get to know my father better now that he was
gone—learning more about this time in his life from the men who
were there with him. Their stories were indirect evidence of what
Dad went through. Who would know more about that than other
soldiers? In speaking to them, I found a way to show my respect
for his service. I could also do this by attending the events, listening to the men's stories, and writing about them.

I began conducting my interviews then, with some of the
men I met that year, whom I also spoke to at subsequent
reunions. Other veterans have been unable to attend the
reunions, so I spoke with them separately.

• • •

At dinner one night that first year, I met Paul Mercer, who had driven his yellow Thunderbird to the reunion all the way from his home in Florida with his daughter Jane. He'd been a part of the 318th, B Company. A wiry man with metallic-gray hair and a weathered face, he had a sharp sense of humor and wise-cracked with the others at the table. Paul, who grew up in New Hampshire, had been a machine gunner during the war. Before he left home to face combat in 1944, his mother gave him a Bible with a steel cover to wear inside his jacket close to his heart. Even though he was never shot, he was convinced that the Bible somehow warded off enemy bullets or mortar shells and kept him alive.

"Almost everybody got hurt or wounded in some way," he said. "It was nearly impossible not to. And you might well get shot by your own people. We got bombed [by the Americans] and we hit the cellars. We knew then what the Germans went through," he chuckled. Then he added, "That happens in war. People make mistakes. Communications break. Get over it and forget it."

Paul was awarded a Purple Heart when he got blown off a railroad track by a high explosive while walking along a railroad bed. Now he often speaks to high school classes about the war and the concentration camp at Ebensee.

When Paul, his daughter, and I sat in his room for the interview, he showed me photos he'd taken at the camp, saying, "You never get used to seeing these pictures. I don't like to look at them, they give me nightmares." He shifted his gaze, rose quickly, and offered to get me a soda or something to eat. I told him that Dad never spoke about seeing Ebensee and that he'd been affected by it, too. Paul's reaction to the photos showed me that Dad's experience was a common one, and even though they'd never met, the two shared a common bond.

I asked him if he spoke about the war now with the men in his unit. "Sure," he said, "we laugh about things—one guy fell into a ditch, another guy fell off a bridge . . . not the disasters so much. Not the slaughters."

The next evening, another veteran—Leroy Pierce—and I pored over Dad's yellowed maps and snippets from his war journal as we lingered at a table in the hall where dinner had been served. His clear explanations and patience helped me as he walked me through what was happening and where Dad's unit was at a particular time. Leroy's war story turned out to be as different from Dad's as it could be.

Leroy joined the Army from his small town in Iowa. His country was at war, and that was all the reason he needed. A private assigned to L Company of the 317th Regiment, he came across the Atlantic as part of the late summer 1944 wave of 80th Division infantryman. In the fierce battle of the Moselle River, the 317th made several attempts at a river crossing on September 5, 1944, facing a determined enemy and horrendous weather. They arrived on the other side of the river in pitch darkness. "At morning light [on September 6], we prepared to make a charge when we heard the word 'surrender' from the area that held our officers," recalled Pierce. "We thought the *Germans* were surrendering. But when they came at us with their machine guns, that quickly changed our minds."

Eighty-nine enlisted men and two officers from L Company were captured. GIs filed by with their hands up, and they all crowded into a nearby barn when, to their shock, American planes commenced a bombardment. After the first hit, the two American officers took whatever white cloths they could find and ran outside in a frantic effort to signal the planes to stop the bombing, but it was too late. "The officers were still waving their white flags when a second hit destroyed the barn." Leroy said. Many were killed or wounded; one of the officers who'd tried to save them was among the fatalities.

The captive GIs were herded off to Stalag VII-A, a POW camp twenty-two miles northeast of Munich and a half-mile south of Moosburg, Germany. The narrow rows of rundown, one-story military barracks in the camp were designed to house 10,000 people, but they held many more. During this time, Leroy gave up smoking so he could trade cigarettes for something more valuable, like warm, heavy pants. He'd been captured wearing his summer cottons, and the unheated barracks were freezing in the fast approaching German winter.

On New Year's Eve, some prisoners at the camp put on a show they'd been preparing in secret. When the men's voices rose to sing "Silent Night" for the opener, tough but homesick soldiers shed tears. Light moments followed where some of the prisoners dressed as women and wore makeup. Although they all enjoyed the show, Leroy said that when it ended, it was back to reality. "Once the curtain came down, you remembered where you were."

After the New Year, Leroy was moved to a much smaller camp some miles away where they put him to work cutting timber. The lowest point in his captivity came the day some German soldiers arrived at the timber camp wearing American uniforms. Leroy and his fellow POWs were stunned at the sight—the Germans would have had to obtain the uniforms from either captured or dead Americans. It was a sign, they thought, that the war was going badly for the Alllies.

On April 29, 1945, about twenty-five American soldiers belonging to a motorized unit were making their way through the forest and happened upon the timber camp. The POWs were even more surprised than the soldiers at the encounter. Although the prisoners weren't aware that the war was coming to an end, the Germans guards were, and they consequently put up no resistance. The trucks approached, the GIs stopped, looked at the POWs, and asked them what they were doing there. The Americans easily gained control of the situation, took the Germans into custody, and prepared to remove the Allied prisoners from the camp.

Most American POWs have worse memories than Leroy does. "I was lucky that the people who ran the camp were not brutal," said Leroy, "as they were in other camps, and that I wasn't wounded. I'm a strong person, solid. I had a good family life before I went, that helped me a lot." It is easy to imagine that Leroy's inner strength and calm served him well.

He also considers himself fortunate not to have endured a long winter and spring of combat, and he expressed sympathy for the soldiers who did. After reading my father's war journal, Leroy said, "Did your dad have spells where he went off by himself? It's a wonder he got out with his sanity intact."

• • •

I enjoyed talking with Paul and Leroy, but I was sad to think I might never find anyone at the reunion who had known my father during the war. Then I found Clayton Warman and George Anderson. I was sitting alone at breakfast on the second morning, reading the local newspaper, when I saw them talking at another table. Clayton had snowy white hair and a ruddy complexion with eyes full of kindness and intelligence. George was a soft-spoken man whose face broke easily into a wide smile.

I recognized something familiar in their bearing. "These two could have been Dad's friends," I thought. But then I spied their nametags, which said 318–F Company, not E, and my heart sank. Still, I followed my gut instinct, and after breakfast

I cornered them in the hallway, introduced myself, and told them I was writing a book about my father, Bill Elvin. Had they known him, by any chance? They mulled it over for a second, then Clayton looked at George and said, "Bill Elvin? From Frostburg? He was our company commander after the war. He was a newspaperman, wasn't he? Oh, yes, we spent a lot of time together. We shared quarters."

Up until then, I hadn't even known that Dad had been in command of a company or that he'd been transferred to F Company after the end of the war in Europe. This information plus the fact that they'd known Dad made the trip to the reunion instantly worthwhile for me. Clayton and George had met Dad on June 19, 1945, when he took command of F Company at the beginning of the American occupation of Germany and Czechoslovakia. "The time your dad joined our Company as commander was a quiet period," Clayton remembered. "We just wanted the whole thing to be over. We were just waiting to go home or else be shipped to Japan."

George was a BAR (Browning Automatic Rifle) man during the war, one of the most hazardous jobs in the infantry. Clayton rose rapidly through the ranks. After the Battle of the Bulge in January 1945, he was promoted from private first class to staff sergeant. Then he got a battlefield commission in March and by mid-May 1945, he was promoted to first lieutenant. "If the war had gone on another year I could have been a general," he joked.

"I remember the day Clayton got his [officer's] commission," recalled Bob Fasnacht, another F Company soldier. "He came back into the barracks and we all crowded around to see the gold bars. He was so respected by everyone, we all wanted to be the first to salute him."

I'd asked Bob several times if he remembered my father and he always said no. But then, one evening he was telling me about life in the Army after V-E Day, explaining that when F

Company was in Kempten, Germany, he'd been in charge of the company newsletter. I told him he and Dad had something in common, because Dad had gone on to become a newspaper-man after the war ended. Bob stopped in midsentence, looked at me, and said excitedly, "*Now* I remember your father! He reamed my ass once about something I'd written! Oh, yes, I re-member him."

At first I was a little taken aback because people usually had only nice things to say about Dad. But it made me laugh. Great! Dad's human. And I knew if there were anything my father would ream someone's ass about, it would be sloppy news re-porting. Dad spent time that summer of 1945 writing up his war journal, between company commander duties. Autumn ushered in crisp, clear weather as F Company left Germany, but the business of war was unfinished. The Company became part of the Army of Occupation in Czechoslovakia (or, as my then almost three-year-old brother Jay told people at home in Cum-berland, "the Army of Czechoslovakiapation").

While in Luhov, Czechoslovakia, on October 4, 1945, five months after the end of the war in Europe, Dad wrote a letter to his parents, commenting on the cold and complaining about Army bureaucracy. He wrote:

> Life in Kempten was not unpleasant, from the military
> standpoint, but Colonel [James] Luckett has gone home and
> things have changed. Not one of these men is interested in
> staying in the Army and a great many of them should be home
> or in civilian life within six months but the strictest regular
> Army standards are being imposed on them. Right at the
> moment the whole regiment is more than slightly disgusted. I'm
> more than tired of this but it can't go on much longer.

He ended by teasing his teetotaler mother: "Now that your [summer] garden is a thing of the past you can divert yourselves by putting alcohol in the car. 'Prestone' is probably a WCTU-inspired [Women's Christian Temperance Union] pseudonym but don't kid yourself, there's alcohol in that snug car you ride to church."

Reading that letter made me wish my own mother had kept Dad's letters from the war. He wrote to her often, but none of the letters survive. Those letters, more than anything else, might have shown his sweeter and more vulnerable side. Missing her and in mortal danger, worrying about leaving her a widow and my brother fatherless, he probably poured his heart out. But Mom destroyed them, so I'll never know. They were hers to throw out, but I longed to have read them.

Finally, the day came in January 1946 when the 80th Infantry Division began its long journey home. The voyage back to the United States took twenty days. George Anderson said the crossing was so rough he was as frightened then as he ever was in combat, and at times he doubted whether he'd make it. The weather in January in the North Atlantic, he said, is the worst weather in the world. "One day it was so rough we covered zero distance—just going up and down in the middle of the ocean," George said. "Every once in awhile you'd get out of synch and you'd come down—bam!"

By the third reunion I attended, in 2007, George, Clayton, Bob, and the rest of F Company had "adopted" me as a daughter. Ever since George and Clayton told me that Dad had been their company commander from June to October 1945, and since E Company had no reunion group of its own, I'd been welcomed into the F Company family and even invited to their meetings.

I was honored to sit in when they pondered what to do with the "Last Man Bottle," or *tontine*. *Tontine* is a French word meaning "pledge." The man who outlives the rest of his company pledges to drink a toast to the friends of his youth, the men who fought by his side. The bottle is typically acquired soon after the war, then kept by one of the members until only the last man remains.

According to legend, the Last Man Bottle tradition in the United States started with the Civil War, when a group of soldiers from the First Battle of Bull Run formed a Last Man Club. They pledged to assemble annually until only one was left and put a bottle of Burgundy into a rosewood box. In July 1930, the Last Man opened the bottle of wine, poured his glass, and recited, as his club had specified long ago:

> *The camp fire smoulders—ashes jail*
> *The clouds are black athwart the sky*
> *No tap of drums, no bugle call*
> *My comrades, all, goodbye.*

F Company's Last Man Club was formed at their reunion in Florida in 1987, when Harry Dunivan, one of the thirty-two men in attendance, bought a bottle of German wine, and Company member Lou Ungar made a handsome wooden case in which to store it. But at the 2007 reunion, the nine members of the F Company Last Man Club in attendance decided to break with tradition and open the bottle so they could share it together. When they opened the bottle, however, they found the wine had turned to vinegar, so they poured the contents down the drain, saved the bottle, and placed it back in its case. But they still wanted to uphold some of the tradition: A bottle needed to be drunk. A new bottle of whiskey soon appeared and, after presenting it to ranking members Ed McDonald and Clayton Warman, they passed it around for a ceremonial drink. As a "family" member, I also took a swig.

• • •

I was not able to interview all the soldiers in that camaraderie of group whiskey drinking. Walter Carr had never attended a reunion, although his presence was felt. When his name came up in conversation among the veterans, it was usually accompanied by an admiring comment about his role in the breakthrough to Bastogne to make first contact with the trapped 101st Airborne.

I interviewed the legendary Lieutenant Carr at his home in Florida, where he stood a bit shorter than his wartime height of 6'3", but his voice was firm and his opinions clear. Walter shared his theory about bravery with me: The brave are more self-confident because they've bonded with their fathers, which provides them with the assurance that they will survive. He mentioned several times that my father had more confidence than he had. Walter said Dad took too many chances and was lucky he was wounded or he would have been killed, but it sounded to me like Walter was talking more about himself than about Dad. He described a Bill Elvin who was a risk taker, almost reckless in his bravery. I didn't know what to make of that, since no one who knew my father would describe him as reckless. I have no doubt that he was courageous in battle and in caring for his men, but reckless? Was the Bill Elvin that Lieutenant Carr knew a different man from the one I knew? And Walter surely underestimated his own bravery.

Walter was a key figure to me, not only because of his heroism during the war and his particular role in the Battle of the Bulge, but also because he was the one living person I knew of who remembered my father in combat, and remembered him well. War veterans make a clear distinction between the soldiers with whom they endured battle conditions—their "band of brothers"—and the rest. Even after Dad became the company commander of F Company after V-E Day, he always identified himself with E Company, where he and Walter had served together.

Wounded three times by January 1945, Walter was entitled to a noncombat assignment but refused to take it. He said, "I was an infantryman. I was scared as hell every time I went out on an attack, but I was not going to be a coward, so I told them to please send me back to Easy Co., 318th Regiment, the 80th Division. That's where I was supposed to be."

He brought back the parachutes he'd used as camouflage to sneak into Bastogne in the snow, and his wife made a nightgown out of them. After the war, Walter told me, he had no nightmares.

• • •

Other soldiers were not so lucky after the war. Wariness, lack of trust, and aversion to noise and crowds were symptoms many soldiers displayed. One told me he had trouble going to restaurants and family gatherings, and he admitted that his behavior toward his family was often harsh and critical.

I wondered how much I had in common with other daughters of World War II soldiers. Did we share a legacy of "the inaccessible father"? Every growing girl has a need to be firmly visible to the world, and her father's approval provides the basis for the shape and individuality she carries into the community. I'm very grateful for a father who wasn't abusive or cruelhearted, but he was remote enough, certainly during my adolescence, to have created an unfulfilled longing in me to be seen and heard. The rare nod of approval, or the comments like "you're coming out of your awkward stage, dear," were not enough and left me feeling hollow. But Dad was a very sensitive man who did love me. He gave me so much, but he was unable to grant me the affirmation of his esteem and love when I needed it most.

But, of course, my father lived to come home to his family. And for that I was, and am, the most grateful of all. When I first interviewed Bill Kelly, Jr., son of Lieutenant Bill Kelly, 318-F, it occurred to me that there was a solemn category of soldier that I had omitted—those who had no homecoming at all. Kelly was one of those whom A. E. Housman, one of Dad's favorite poets, referred to as "the lads that will die in their glory and never be old" in his poem "A Shropshire Lad."

Kelly was a passionate Irishman, an accomplished athlete, and an especially avid golfer. In the evenings at his home in Madison, Wisconsin, he would putt in the living room after work while smoking his pipe. He'd emigrated to the United States from Canada as a teenager, having been brought up poor on a farm in Saskatchewan, and joined the National Guard in 1936. He married and took up work with the power company. Bill Jr. was born in 1938.

Kelly left the States on October 22, 1944, for England, and then he promptly shipped out to France to join F Company. Captain Ed McDonald, the company commander, met the new lieutenant for the first time on November 24, the night before Kelly led a platoon into action near Zimming, France, east of the Moselle River. Kelly told McDonald that night about the wife and young son he'd left behind in Madison, and then they went on to discuss the upcoming battle and plans for Kelly to take over one of the platoons.

The next morning saw a ferocious battle, the assault on the Maginot Line, a series of concrete fortifications built by the French to defend against the Germans. The Battalion attacked at 8 A.M. and was met with heavy artillery and mortar fire. A man ran up to McDonald and said, "One of the lieutenants is badly wounded." The captain went over and saw that Kelly had a serious chest wound that looked like the result of a mortar shell. He tried to hurry up the medics, but too many soldiers had been wounded. The medics were doing the best they could.

It took seventeen days for the first of two telegrams to arrive on Oak Street in Madison, Wisconsin. Bill Jr. recalls the date of the first one—December 12, 1944. "Lieutenant William P. Kelly was wounded in battle. Word will follow." There was a frantic rush to find out where he was and if he was still alive. Three long and agonizing days later, his mother opened the door to receive the second telegram. Bill Jr. clung to her leg as she read the telegram and fell back from the door, crying, "Oh, no, oh no." She staggered back but Bill wouldn't let go.

Christmas came and went with no tree and no celebration. Young Bill's sole present was a cap from Camp Croft, South Carolina, where his dad had trained. He wondered why everyone insisted on consoling him. Something terrible had happened, he knew, because family and friends were crying, but he was only six—too young to grasp the finality of his father's death.

In the months and years that followed, he would sneak into the drawer where his mother kept his father's letters. He'd read them when everyone was gone. When his mother watched news clips from World War II on television, Bill Jr. sat riveted, searching for his father in the sea of soldiers' faces.

His mother put away the picture of Lieutenant Kelly that she had kept on top of the tall Bendix radio and tried to close the book on that chapter of her life. She stopped talking to her son about him, remarried, and never told Bill Jr. the details of his father's death. Bill Jr. was a reminder of the husband and father the family had lost, and she and her new husband wanted to move beyond those memories.

Like his father, Bill Jr. was a superb high school athlete, but his mother and stepfather never came to his track meets or football games. His two new sisters got most of the attention. "I felt boxed out of that deal," he says, referring to his mother's "new family." He remembers her telling someone she had two daughters. He said, "What about me, Mom?" She replied, laughing, "Oh, I forgot about you, Bill."

Several soldiers who knew his father only briefly have contacted him over the years to say what a fine man he was. One fellow soldier who'd struck up a friendship with Lieutenant Kelly aboard ship contacted Bill Jr. through the 80th Division fifty years later because he had always wondered what happened to Kelly after he arrived in France. "You're with a guy for five days and you remember him for fifty years?" said Bill Jr. in awe.

Captain McDonald never forgot him either. After the war, McDonald went on to become the president of Shell Oil Mexico. After he retired from Shell Oil, he was asked to do a project by the energy office of the state of Connecticut in 1988. He became friends there with Tom Fitzpatrick, a Korean War veteran, and their lunches together became opportunities to ruminate over life in the infantry during wartime. When McDonald mentioned a young lieutenant in his company from Madison, Wisconsin, who'd been killed in action, he learned that Fitzpatrick was also from Madison. Fitzpatrick remembered that a young lieutenant on his block had been killed in the war, and the name "Kelly" rang a bell. After several phone calls to the old neighborhood, he and McDonald were amazed to find that the Bill Kelly who'd lived on Fitzpatrick's block and the Bill Kelly who'd spent his last night alive talking with Ed McDonald were one and the same. McDonald wasted no time in establishing communication with Bill Jr., who was by then grown and living in California with a wife and two sons. The two met and sat down together, and McDonald told Bill Jr. the story of his father's last night, the night he'd talked about his wife and son.

Some years later, Bill Jr. went to visit his father's grave in the peaceful quiet of the military cemetery in St. Avold, France. Having been told where his father's body rested among the 10,000 American soldiers buried there, he drove in, parked his car, glanced down the long row, and somehow walked right up to his father's gravestone.

The hurtful effects of his father's death and his isolation from his family as a child have been painful for Bill Jr. His mother's refusal to talk to him as a child about his father still rankles. "Once in awhile she would crease the edge of it, but then she'd withdraw," he said. He still has the picture of his father that his mother once kept on top of the radio and kissed every night before she went to bed. But there are no pictures of the two of them, father and son, together.

"I didn't get emotional about it until the last quarter of my life," he said. He is sure that if his father had survived, he would have been awarded a medal or two for his bravery. "He would have done well," he said. "The 318th didn't give away too many medals, but he would have earned them."

Lieutenant Kelly didn't come back alive, nor did 3,038 others from the 80th Infantry Division. Since then, many of them, like my father, have died from illness or accidents. But as long as there remains a "last man," a spark of this band of brothers lives on.

CHAPTER ELEVEN

The Box from Braunau

"I Am Done With War"
—The title of a poem by Bill Elvin, age 17

The silvery-white box has lost its moonlight sheen, its patina mottled and dimmed by time. Judging by the drawing of a man and woman surrounded by flowers on its top, its craftsman was a romantic. Judging by his writing, "Braunau 1944" (birthplace of Adolf Hitler) on one side, he was also not without a sense of history.

The Germans, in their march to take over Western Europe, forced millions of able men and women into arduous labor to further their regime. Was he one of the young people swept off the streets of his home in a conquered country by the Nazi war machine, too strong and too useful to send to an extermination camp? Most likely, he had smuggled the materials to make the box out of the aluminum factory in Braunau during the long days he toiled there before returning each night to his fenced-in prison. He must have wondered what kind of future he would have, or whether he would have a future at all.

Dad had told me that the man had given him the box because he was so thankful to be liberated by the American soldiers. The gesture of the gift, representing a captive's yearning for freedom, symbolized what the Allied soldiers were fighting for. But to my father, the box was a daily reminder of the victims of Nazi tyranny. Dad knew that without the sacrifices that had been made, millions and millions more—in addition to the box-maker in Braunau and the inmates at Ebensee—would have been enslaved and slaughtered.

After he finally left Braunau, did the maker of the box ever wonder about Dad? What would he have thought if he'd known that my father kept his tiny childhood Bible, along with his Purple Heart, Silver Star, and Combat Infantryman's Badge, in the box for many years, and that it meant so much to him that he gave it to my brother George for safekeeping?

If I had not seen the box at George's house in 2003 and had Ursula not insisted I investigate its origins, Dad's silence about the war might never have been broken. Throughout the writing of this book, the metaphor of the box has served as a guide for me: opening, revealing, and healing.

• • •

In the summer of 2006, two years after my father's death, I returned to Frostburg to take another look at the houses Dad had lived in, to eat lunch at the Princess Restaurant he had loved, and simply to breathe the mountain air he'd breathed. I decided to take in the Frostburg Museum, housed in a building dating back to 1899 that had once been the Hill Street schoolhouse. At the time of my visit, one sizable room was dedicated to the history of local schools and was filled with row after row of small desks like schoolrooms of old.

Betty Van Newkirk, the delightful curator of the Frostburg Museum Association and a Frostburg historian (who was then ninety years old), showed me into the musty room and invited me to have a seat. I eyed the small wooden desks, wondering if

I would be able to slip into one of them with any gracefulness, and managed to slide in from the side. I told Mrs. Van Newkirk about my father and the book I was writing and that I was looking for anything that would shed light on what kind of boy Dad had been. My anticipation grew as we pored over old yearbooks, tattered programs from school plays, and memorabilia from those days. I spied Dad's serious yet boyish face as it looked out at me with a steady gaze from the yellowed pages of the Beall High School Class of 1935 yearbook. I saw a handsome young man, innocent, idealistic, and a bit full of himself. (This was, as he'd said, "another year of greatness.")

Digging into another drawer, Mrs. Van Newkirk pulled out a book of poetry written by the high school students and handed it to me. When I opened it, one poem by "Elvin, W. J., Jr." jumped out.

A jolt shot through my body when I saw the title: "I Am Done With War." The coincidence was stark. My father had written an antiwar poem when he was only seventeen, seven years before he enlisted in the Army. And here I was, writing a book about his experiences during World War II. Mrs. Van Newkirk was almost as excited as I was at what we'd found. I began to read.

I Am Done With War

I lost a boy at Verdun,
Oh, how happy he was to leave!
Before starting, his race was run,
And alone, I was left to grieve.

And yet, I would like to go
To Japan or perhaps back to France,
For I love the exciting flow
Of men in the first advance.

But years ago, I went back;
Saw those markers all over the hill
Yes, someone had shot my son
And forgotten, "Thou shalt not kill."

So, I am done with war,
The lust, and the blood, and the stench;
Yes, I am done with war.
Give me the hearth for the trench.

Noting his description of a father who mourns the loss of his son at the Battle of Verdun during World War I it struck me as ironic that Dad's relationship with his own firstborn son had suffered from his absence and the emotional toll of war. Like a broken bone that fails to knit properly, their relationship never healed.

What had caused the break between Dad and Jay in the first place? Surrounded by our mother and both sets of devoted grandparents, Jay's early life had been idyllic, even without his father. Then, just after his third Christmas, Dad returned from Europe and, of course, took control of the father role immediately. But their separation in Jay's early years and Dad's need to impose authority over our family life may have laid the groundwork for their difficult relationship.

My father had been made to grow up fast and, now that the intense drama of war was over, more huge adjustments were required. As the family tried to remake its life together, the grisly details of wartime were creeping through Dad's veins. His experience mirrored that of many infantrymen: He'd been shot at, wounded, hospitalized, and sent back to the front to be shot at again. The medals awarded him attested to his courage, but the experience had taken its toll. He didn't even talk about it to his own father, who had not seen combat in World War I because he'd been raising his own siblings after his parents died. Ultimately, Dad found no one to share his wartime experiences with. And, as Robert Abzug says about those who saw the concentration camps, "The sights and smells of the liberated camps were hard enough to grasp and assimilate when on the scene. It would be difficult in the extreme to convey that reality second-hand to those at home."[1]

The relationships men forged in wartime were based, in part, on mutual protection, survival, and shared experiences. When Dad returned from the war, the memory of those deep connections may have overshadowed his family relationships and further alienated him from those he loved who loved him.

• • •

In Frostburg, I looked out the tall windows of the museum onto Hill Street. Mrs. Van Newkirk had gone off to respond to another request for help, leaving me alone to absorb what I had found. Off in the distance I could see the blue hazy backdrop of the Western Maryland mountains behind the gently sloping hills of the Frostburg Memorial Park, where Dad's grave lay. My mind wandered back to that warm August afternoon two years earlier when we had buried him. Surrounded by friends and family, I had felt the weight and pleasure that comes with shared history and place of belonging. The peaks of the Allegheny Mountain range had cradled both my parents through their childhood and held them in a protective hollow to which Dad would often return; it soothed his wounds and mended his heart. That area often felt like home to me, too.

My cousin Kate, a Presbyterian minister who gave the eulogy at Dad's graveside, had handed each family member a spray of heather to place on top of the coffin before it was lowered into the ground. She'd just returned from Scotland and had brought the heather with her, not knowing she would be offering it for this purpose.

"A son of the land of the mountain and the mist," was how my grandfather Jim often identified himself, speaking of Scotland. But I knew when the mist gathered around the gravestones that morning, the phrase could refer to Western Maryland as well, tying the two together. Dad had come back here once again, not to some terrible place—not to Ebensee, where he had seen horrors; nor Rouves, where he was wounded; nor the hospital in England; nor our front lawn the day Mom left—but to the other "land of mountain and mist," his true home.

From my desk in the museum, I pondered the trajectory of his life from the moment of birth, when the bells rang at Greyfriars Church in Dumfries, to Georgie's death and Dad's accomplishments during his early life. Then came his life-changing experiences in World War II I'd since learned about. I reflected on his career as a newspaperman and warmed with pride, silently appreciating the deep and authentic contributions he'd made to his community. I thought of his long marriage to my beautiful mother, pictured her laughing and imagined them when they were happy together. I felt the familiar ache in my gut when I thought of their divorce, but that was followed by the breath of relief that came when I thought of Ruth and my father's final, happy years.

I considered the mistakes I'd made and the regrets I had, which included failing to ask him more about his war sooner. To try to make up for it, I'd traveled far to fill in the gaps since his death—to Austria, back to Maryland, and to 80th Infantry Division reunions I'd attended in Ohio, Georgia, and Pennsylvania. Each interview, letter, and conversation had expanded my perspective on him. Each step I took to learn more about his life brought me closer to breaking the invisible barriers between us.

Sometimes people forget how much fathers mean to their daughters. I adored my father, and something about returning to Frostburg that summer of 2006 produced a flood of memories: Dad singing to me, walking around holding babies George and Marty while talking to the birds outside, flashing his wonderful grin, always being gracious, reciting poetry, and, of course, rescuing my little red tennis shoe.

What had I learned about him? Like Robert Graves in *Good-Bye to All That*, my father must have vowed after the war that he would never be subject to anyone's orders again. It was so important to him to be independent, to branch out from the *Washington Star* and to fulfill his dream of owning and editing a weekly newspaper.

Duty and loyalty counted for a lot, and he showed it by writing a letter to his parents every Sunday of their lives. He remained concerned about my mother as well and, I believe, felt "married" to her until her death, even though they were divorced for nearly as many years as they were married. He was a firm friend to everyone, including people in trouble or down on their luck. And instilled in him by his parents was the conviction that life expected good things from him rather than the other way around.

He spent his life bringing information to people, observing human behavior and actions, and making sense of events. He'd written eloquently in his journal about his first experiences with combat, but after he was wounded, he never picked up his pen (or went to his typewriter) again to write about the meat grinder he'd been through.

When my cousin Kate spoke about Dad at his interment, she called him "a disciplined intellectual, a student of the word. Always the penchant for writing—and rewriting—his father's son with files upon files that one day might prove useful and always were. Prepared for this task, he was never without five or six pencils or pens, tools of his trade." Even though words were his stock-in-trade, all the pens and pencils in the world couldn't help him write or find a place to file the ghastly information about the atrocities he saw in the camps.

At the beginning of this book, I said that the process of researching and writing had opened the door for our family to heal, and I hoped that would happen. But I'm not sure it did for anyone but Dad and me; I can't speak for the rest of the family. It's up to each person to interpret and transform his or her own life's story. Carl Jung had it right when he said it all depends on how we look at things, not on how they were.

• • •

During the Civil War, what is now termed post-traumatic stress disorder was touchingly called "soldier's heart." During World War I, it changed to "shell shock," then in World War II to "combat fatigue," and after Vietnam it came to be called PTSD. I was surprised to find how strongly PTSD symptoms matched up with behavior my father had exhibited—behavior that had mystified me all these years. All of a sudden, it began to fit. The pieces of the "What happened to Dad?" puzzle were coming together. I saw the connection between the man who'd written about the fright and panic of mortar artillery fire—"tight, tight, tight, and down, down, down"—and his tamped-down emotions. It was more—to use the clinical terms—the hypervigilance, the exaggerated startle response, the need to control, and the disassociation. I could see now that his habit of suddenly changing the subject, his jumping out of his skin when surprised, his need to tell *us* what *we* needed, were all symptomatic of PTSD.

His intellect and sensitivity, along with his inner struggle to keep anxiety at bay, combined to create a complex man, full of ironies. While sometimes he could be sarcastic and cutting, no one would say he was unkind.

I could not have written this book while he was alive because I would have worried about his approval. And, unmoored as I was in some ways by his death, I was surprised to see that it allowed me to get to know him more deeply than while he lived. As the playwright Robert Anderson said, "death ends a life; it does not end a relationship." The conversation we began shortly before his death continues.

My father always kept the worst tales to himself, though. In this, my family is not alone. In fact, many veterans have gone to their graves without their families ever knowing they were concentration camp liberators. Although it's the combat veterans who spend the rest of their lives paying for the war long after it's ended, their families are often war casualties as well.

Although World War II takes us back to a simpler time, when enemies could be identified and our cause was unambiguously righteous, it was unquestionably a horrifyingly brutal war. All wars leave permanent psychological marks on the soldiers who fight them, and World War II was no exception, despite its misnomer, "The Good War." Veterans now returning from the Middle East share the recurring nightmares and shattered nerves that plagued veterans of World War II, Vietnam, and other wars. Many of their children have been warned, as we were in my family, not to rouse their fathers or mothers suddenly or startle them. If suddenly awakened, they might fail to distinguish a child from a Viet Cong, a German SS, or an insurgent in Iraq.

The *Washington Post* periodically publishes the names and photographs of American soldiers killed in Afghanistan and Iraq, along with their unit and the circumstances of their death. I've sat down with the newspaper on those days, looking at each of those photos and reading about the men and women who have sacrificed and died. Many are younger than my twenty-four-year-old son. I think of those whose lives have been cut short, their stricken families, and I hope and pray for the safe return of their comrades.

With World War II behind us, it's possible to calculate the numbers of survivors, of wounded, of missing and dead, but those figures never tell the whole story. Now that the men of the 80th Infantry Division have welcomed me into their family circle—I'm the daughter of one of their own—my connection to the narrative of World War II has changed forever. For my part, I am privileged to know them. Even my outlook on the military has changed and become more positive. It took these friendships for me, a child of the antiwar and anti-military 1960s, to truly understand that the soldier or the veteran is rarely eager to enter into a war. The soldier knows best what is at stake.

•   •   •

The air outside the Frostburg Museum had grown still as the storm clouds gathered. Before I packed up my things to leave, I took a moment to look back one more time at the events of the day the last time I'd come to Frostburg in August 2004.

The moment had come to lay Dad to rest. We gathered close together to listen as the lone bagpiper played a haunting version of Dvorak's "Going Home" from atop the next rise. Then, just as the bagpiper's notes faded and Dad was lowered down next to Georgie, Jim, and Annie, a peal of church bells from the town rang out over the hillside. My brother George leaned over to me, eyes shining, and whispered, "Hear them? The church bells, just like when he was born."

NOTE

1. Robert H. Abzug, *Inside the Vicious Heart: Americans and the Liberation of Nazi Concentration Camps* (New York: Oxford University Press, 1985), p. 127.

AFTERWORD

"No set of laws or Bill of Rights for returning veterans of combat can do [the] job. Only their own people can do it. So it is very important that these people know and understand combat men."

—Bill Mauldin, *Up Front* (1945)

Common elements in the drama of a soldier returning home have been repeated many times: first the daydreams, the anticipation, and the ecstatic reunions. Then the quiet tiptoes in, sometimes followed by nightmares, alienation, and loneliness. Soldiers aren't the only casualties of war; their families suffer as well, although their battles are fought later, on the home front.

After a long separation, family members may be confused by a veteran's distant and controlling behavior as he or she attempts to adjust to life out of the combat zone. Your father or another loved one may have served and fought in World War II, like mine, or perhaps in Korea, Vietnam, the Gulf War, Afghanistan, or Iraq. Regardless of where the fighting took place, does your veteran speak of it sparingly and then fall silent?

Reading this book may help you to sit down and talk together, and in turn encourage you to begin a search for more information about his or her war. After researching my father's time overseas, finding men with whom he'd fought and accounts of actions in which he'd been involved, I'm now able to offer some advice on how to go about your own pursuit. In particular, be aware that the men and women who served in World War II are dying at a rate of 1,100 each day, so our time with them is very limited. Their buddies may still be alive, and the appendices that follow provide some help on how to locate them. Even if your parent, uncle, or grandparent has passed away, learning what happened to him in his war can be both rewarding and comforting.

To veterans and civilians alike, my father's firsthand accounts of combat may make for gripping reading and may spark memories for any combat veteran. Dad's journal and life story are valuable not only to anyone interested in the World War II but to those who know someone affected by war, whether his behavior pointed to PTSD or not. And in this respect, perhaps his story can be used as a guide.

I cannot say whether my father would have been clinically diagnosed with PTSD, but he certainly displayed a majority of the symptoms. As I stated previously, from the time as children we learned never to sneak up on my father or surprise him with a loud noise, I knew that "something *happened* to Dad," as Scott Turow says in his novel *Ordinary Heroes*. But it wasn't until I found the box from Braunau that I began to unravel just what that was.

Our family's early difficulties with Dad cannot be understood apart from the symptoms of PTSD that he exhibited: the heightened alertness, the avoidance, the anxieties, nightmares, and flashbacks. If you have experienced something similar with your loved one, you're not alone, and I suspect our experiences are far from rare. After all, my father was hardly an extreme example of what the stress of combat and war can do to a person. He didn't lose his mind, and by most measures, he led a successful life. But he was haunted by the past, and his marriage to my mother and relationship with me and my sister and brothers suffered for it. This book tells a flesh-and-blood story about a man who silently struggled to live in the present but could not forget his past.

The preservation of Dad's part in World War II has been important to me, but beyond that, my goal in writing this book has been to paint a portrait in words of my father that others might recognize—either in themselves, or in someone they know now or knew in the past. Unfortunately, PTSD carries a stigma that even now keeps soldiers quiet about their feelings. The appendices that follow also include material about PTSD.

Anna Quindlen has said that it's the sacrifice of the veterans, not the merits of the war, that we need to remember. This is what makes my father's story transcend time, politics, and geography. It's not just veterans of the so-called "good war" whose stories should be told, but those of more recent, less "popular" wars as well. Learning about our loved ones' experiences won't turn them into pleasant events, but it will deepen our grasp of what they had to endure and may mitigate family conflict.

No one, least of all an elderly veteran, should be pressured to talk about the war if he or she is not willing to do so. But we can do our research and respectfully ask questions. More importantly, we can listen. The rewards of reconciliation, forgiveness, and the love we want may be within our reach.

Army Organization in World War II

The History of the 80th Infantry Division

First organized in 1917, the 80th Infantry Division consisted mostly of men from Pennsylvania, Virginia, and West Virginia. It was called the "Blue Ridge Division" and its insignia carried three blue mountain peaks representing the Blue Ridge Mountains in those states. Its Latin motto is *Vis Montium*, or "strength of the mountains."

The 80th fought in France in World War I, then was deactivated in June 1919. In 1942, the Blue Ridge Division was reactivated in Camp Forrest, Tennessee. In July 1944, the Division set sail aboard the *Queen Mary*, arriving in Scotland on July 7, bringing the number of U.S. infantry divisions in the European Theater of Operations to fourteen.

After crossing the Channel and arriving in Normandy on Utah Beach on August 3, 1944 (D-Day + 58), the 80th fought its way through campaigns of northern France, Ardennes, Rhineland, and Central Europe. The European war ended on May 7, 1945, with the unconditional surrender of German forces, and the 80th remained in Europe until January 1946 to maintain peace and restore order.

The Army Table of Organization

The following description uses my father's particular units as examples.

- *Army,* commanded by a lieutenant general or full general
  Third Army, consisting of several Corps and Divisions
- *Corps,* commanded by major generals
  XX Corps
  Made up of three to six Divisions
- *Division,* commanded by major generals
  13,412 men
  80th Infantry Division
  Consisted of three Regiments
- *Regiment,* commanded by colonels
  3,256 men
  318th Regiment
  Consisted of three Battalions
- *Battalion,* commanded by lieutenant colonels
  871 men
  2nd Battalion
  Made up of three Rifle Companies and one Heavy Weapons Company
- *Rifle Company,* commanded by captains
  193 men
  E Company (Easy Company)
  Consisted of three to four platoons
- *Heavy Weapons Company,* commanded by captains
  166 men
  H Company
  Consisted of three to four platoons

- *Platoon*, commanded by lieutenants
  Forty to forty-five men
  Fourth Platoon
  Made up of three to four squads
- *Rifle Squad*, commanded by junior sergeant or corporal
  Twelve men

Definitions

World War II Infantry Division: An infantry division is the largest ground combat formation and normally includes infantry, artillery, and armored components. The company is the main administrative unit of the infantry.

The 80th Division landed on Utah Beach on August 3, 1944 (D-Day + 58), and my father, as a replacement officer, arrived only a few days later. He didn't join up with his regiment, the 318th, until the 80th approached the Moselle River.

Infantry Regiment: The infantry regiment consists of three battalions (1st, 2nd, and 3rd), an anti-tank company, a cannon company, a headquarters company, a service company, and a medical attachment.

Infantry Battalion: Each battalion consists of three or four companies and a headquarters. The 1st Battalion is made up of rifle companies A, B, and C with heavy weapons company D; 2nd Battalion includes rifle companies E, F, and G with heavy weapons company H; and 3rd Battalion of rifle companies I, K, and L, with heavy weapons company M.

Infantry Company: A company is made up of three or four platoons: three infantry platoons, a weapons platoon, and a company HQ for a total of 193 men—six officers and 187 enlisted men. They were lettered sequentially through the regiment: "A" Company, "B" Company, and so on, through "M" Company. The letter "J" was omitted, so it wouldn't be confused with "I" company. They were given names as follows: Able, Baker, Charlie, Dog, Easy, Fox, George, How, Item, King, Love, and Mike, corresponding to the phonetic alphabet to avoid mistakes in transmission of messages.

Infantry Platoon: Platoons are the smallest military unit led by an officer in the Army. A lieutenant, such as my father, would command a platoon, consisting of forty to forty-five men.

Rifle Squad: A rifle squad consisted of twelve men, commanded by a junior sergeant or corporal.

There are numerous other units, such as armored divisions, tank destroyer battalions, and cavalry, which attach to a division during wartime.

Statistics on the 80th Infantry Division for World War II

- Killed in action: 3,038
- Wounded: 12,484
- Missing: 448
- Captured: 1,077
- Total casualties: 17,097
- Days in combat: 277
- Enemy soldiers captured: 212,295

- Medals of Honor: 4
- Distinguished Unit Citations: 6
- Distinguished Service Crosses: 48
- Silver Stars: 671
- Bronze Stars: 3,357

Grateful acknowledgment to the following sources for this material:

Adkins, A. Z. Jr. and Andrew Z. Adkins III. *You Can't Get Much Closer Than This: Combat with Company H, 317th Infantry Regiment, 80th Division.* Havertown, PA: Casemate Publishing, 2005.

Gawne, Jonathan. *Finding Your Father's War: A Practical Guide to Researching and Understanding Service in the World War II US Army.* Drexel Hill, PA: Casemate Publishing, 2006.

My Father's Wartime Itinerary

The following is an approximate list of what my father did during World War II. Many Army records from World War II were destroyed in a fire in St. Louis in 1973, making it difficult to reconstruct timelines and activities. I have pieced this list together from letters, military records that Dad kept, 80th Infantry Division materials, and help from others. Some of the dates are approximate and there are gaps where I could not find the information.

1942

- June: Enlists as a VOC (Volunteer Officer Candidate)
  September 12: reports to Fort Meade, Maryland

- September-December: Trains at Fort Meade, Maryland and Camp Croft, South Carolina

1943

- January-May: Attends Infantry Officer's Training School at Fort Benning, Georgia

April: Returns to Camp Croft and trains with 35th
Infantry Training Battalion

1944

- Continues training at Camp Breckenridge, Kentucky
- July: Leaves for Europe and trains in England and
  Wales
- August 5 (D-Day + 60): Lands in France on Omaha
  Beach
- August 5 to September: Moves from St. Lo, France to
  Moselle River area
- November 3–8: In Seille River area; is wounded on
  November 8
- November 8 to after Christmas: In hospitals in Paris
  and England

1945

- February: Returns to duty; in Sauer River area of
  Luxembourg; crosses the Siegfried Line
- March: Crosses the Rhine River at Rambach,
  Germany
- April 22–29: In Nuremberg, Germany; crosses the
  Danube River
- May 3–6: In Braunau, Austria, participates in the
  liberation of labor camps
- May 8: In Liezen, Austria on Victory in Europe Day
  (V-E Day)

- Mid-May: In Gmunden, Austria, guides the Sixth German Army to the Prisoner of War area; visits concentration camp at KZ-Ebensee, Austria
- June 19: Becomes company commander of F Company, 318th Regiment
- July: In Kempten, Germany
- October 4: In Luhov, Czechoslovakia
- October: Is transferred to the 358th Infantry Regiment, 90th Infantry Division

1946

- January: Takes three-week trip home on a Liberty ship

1953

- June: Terminates Reserves appointment as a captain

Glossary of Terms and Military Acronyms

After Action Report	Compilation of all the individual reports packaged to provide an overview of what the unit did each month.
AEF	Allied Expeditionary Force, the combined forces of the countries fighting the Axis during World War II.
Army of Occupation	Post-war occupation by the U.S. Army of Germany and formerly German-occupied nations.
Battle of the Bulge	A major counteroffensive launched by the Germans on December 6, 1944, in the brutal cold of the Ardennes in Belgium, France, and Luxembourg. At first, it succeeded, forcing a "bulge" in the Allied line, but the Germans were halted within a few weeks.

bridgehead	A position established at a bridge or at the ford of a river in an offensive or defensive action against the enemy.
burp gun	Nickname for lightweight portable submachine gun used in World War II.
concentration camp	A guarded enclosure for the detention or imprisonment of political prisoners, prisoners of war, aliens, and/or refugees. The Nazis established some 15,000 camps in occupied countries.
CP	Command Post.
displaced persons (DPs)	The millions of soldiers and civilians left far from their homelands after World War II. Many were Eastern Europeans who became slave laborers for the Nazis.
ETO	European Theater of Operations, the term that refers to U.S. operations in World War II in Europe and the Mediterranean.
slave labor camps, also called forced labor camps	The camps housing prisoners from concentration camps and workers conscripted in occupied Poland and Ukraine. In forced labor camps, prisoners were compelled to work, on starvation rations, in agriculture, highway building, and factories for the

German state. Labor was also viewed as a form of killing by attrition. Information from the postwar Nuremberg trials estimated that there were 12 million forced laborers, from Belgium, the Netherlands, Luxembourg, France, Denmark, and Norway in the west and from Poland, the Baltic States, Hungary, Romania, and Czechoslovakia in the east.

Kristallnacht   "The Night of Broken Glass," November 9, 1938, the date of a pogrom against the Jews in Germany, in which their homes, synagogues, and businesses were attacked.

KZ, or *Konzentrationslager*   The German acronym and name for concentration camp.

Morning report   Detailed personnel information about the men and activities of each company.

POW   Prisoner of war.

Redoubt   Region in Austria believed at one time by the Allies to be a fortified position to which Hitler might flee and might house food, military supplies and even weapons manufacturing facilities.

SHAEF   Supreme Headquarters Allied Expeditionary Force, the designation for the office of General Dwight D. Eisenhower, the Supreme Commander.

Siegfried Line   Powerful system of concrete and steel fortifications set up by Germans along their western frontier in World War I.

SS   The abbreviation for *Schutzstaffel,* the Protection Forces that started as bodyguards for Adolf Hitler and grew into an organization thought of as the elite cadre of Nazi Germany.

stalag   German for prisoner of war camp. A contraction of *Stammlager.* Used for noncommissioned personnel (for U.S. Army) in World War II.

Wehrmacht   The German armed forces.

Sources

Abzug, Robert H. *Inside the Vicious Heart: Americans and the Liberation of Nazi Concentration Camps.* New York: Oxford University Press, 1985.

Chamberlain, Brewster, and Marcia Feldman, eds. *The Liberation of the Nazi Concentration Camps, 1945: Eyewitness Accounts of the Liberators.* Washington, DC: United States Holocaust Memorial Council, 1987.

Sources for Information on Post-Traumatic Stress Disorder (PTSD) for Veterans

The U.S. Department of Defense (DOD) manages all military health systems, including the Veterans Administration. The current demand for mental healthcare for returning veterans and their families now far exceeds the supply of qualified caregivers. Waiting lists are so long for veterans, their spouses, and especially their children that the DOD has asked the American Psychological Association, for the first time, to help train "civilian" providers to conduct therapy with veterans and their families. (The DOD will certify these providers to take military insurance.) In addition, the DOD recently allocated $25 million to study PTSD in combat veterans, the largest award the department has ever made to study the issue. If you wish to find further information about PTSD for yourself or anyone else, the resources described below are available.

Fact sheets are available from the Department of Veterans Affairs on topics such as "PTSD and the Family," "Symptoms of Post Traumatic Stress Disorders (PTSD)," "Effects of Violence," "PTSD and Older Veterans," "War-Zone–Related

Stress Reactions: What Families Need to Know," and "Children of Veterans and Adults with PTSD." Some of these fact sheets are available only online and can be accessed through the department's website at www.ncptsd.va.gov/ncmain/index.jsp. You can also send an e-mail to mailto:ncptsd @va.gov or call the PTSD information line at 802-296-6300.

Here are other organizations you can contact for information and support:

Sidran Traumatic Stress Institute
200 East Joppa Road, Suite 207
Baltimore, MD 21286
410-825-8888
www.sidran.org

Center for Deployment Psychology
Department of Medical and Clinical Psychology
Uniformed Services University of the Health Sciences
4301 Jones Bridge Road, Bldg. 53-104
Bethesda, MD 20814
301-295-4140
www.deploymentpsych.org

Trauma Survivors Anonymous
2022 Fifteenth Avenue
Columbus, VA 31901
706-649-6500

Military OneSource (a 24/7 counseling service and website)
800-342-9647
www.militaryonesource.com

National Suicide Hotline (available 24/7)
800-273-TALK; press 1 to reach the VA Hotline

Philadelphia Veterans Centers
801 Arch Street, Suite 102
Philadelphia, PA 19107
215-627-0238

How to Search for Your Father's War

Books and Websites

The best place to start searching for your father's war is with Jonathan Gawne's book *Finding Your Father's War: A Practical Guide to Researching and Understanding Service in the World War II US Army* (Drexel Hill, PA: Casemate Publishing, 2006). Gawne limits his book to the U.S. Army largely because most World War II Army records were destroyed in a fire in 1973, so Army records are difficult to find. (In contrast, Navy and Marine records are easy to retrieve.) Gawne's book is thorough and covers topics such as how to understand the way the Army is organized, how to decide what records you need and want, and how to access a veteran's records. The companion website to Gawne's book is www.fatherswar.org.

Dad's War: Finding and Telling Your Father's World War II Story is a large and very helpful website with links to many sites pertaining to World War II. The site is at members.aol.com/dadswar.

The U.S. Army Center of Military History website is at

www.history.army.mil/. The Center of Military History makes available a library collections of documents, references, and oral histories to private researchers.

For information on POWs and MIAs from World War II, you can read the 1992–1996 Findings of the World War II Working Group at aiipowmia.com/wwii/wwiiwkgrp.html.

Research Sites

The United States World War II Memorial website lists veterans who have visited the memorial or put information about themselves on the Web page. I found quite a few veterans through this site, which maintains a registry. The memorial is located on 17th Street in between Constitution and Independence Avenues in Washington, DC. For more information call 202-619-7222 or go to http://www.nps.gov/nwwm.

The United States Army Heritage & Education Center, located in Carlisle, Pennsylvania, is the Army's primary historical research facility with a very large collection of personal papers from U.S. Army soldiers in World War II. Their staff keeps a sign on the Information Desk that says "Please Disturb." The website is www.carlisle.army.mil/ahec and the telephone number is 717-245-3971.

The National Archives and Records Administration has collections of World War II photos, unit records, *After Action Reports*, unit histories, military service records, and photos. They are located right outside Washington, DC, in College Park, Maryland. The website is www.archives.gov and the telephone number is 866-272-6272.

The United States Holocaust Memorial Museum, located in Washington, DC, has records about concentration camps liberated by U.S. soldiers, including personal testimonies about the liberations by both soldiers and prisoners. The site is at www.ushmm.org and the telephone number is 202-488-0400.

The Veterans History Project at the Library of Congress, Washington, DC, seeks to preserve stories of wartime service by any veteran. You can browse the website to search for others in your veteran's unit. You can also learn how to become part of the Project. If you go to the Library of Congress, you can see videotapes of veterans telling their stories, some of which have been put on the website at www.loc.gov/vets. The telephone number is 202-707-4916.

NPRC—National Personnel Records Center lost many individual records of World War II veterans in a fire in 1973. They do have *Morning Reports* from World War II companies, which cannot be found at the National Archives. Their address is 9700 Page Avenue, St. Louis, MO, 3132-5100. The telephone number is 314-801-0800, and their website address is http://www.archives.gov/st-louis/.

When planning a visit to any of these places, always check the website or call first. Each has specific requirements on visits.

If your veteran was a member of the 80th Infantry Division, you are fortunate because you will find much useful information on its website (http://www.80thdivision.com) thanks to Andy Adkins. Andy, descendant of a veteran of the 80th, is helping to preserve the history of the division by digitizing both the *Morning Reports* and *After Action Reports* and making them available online. The site is at 80thdivision.com/WebArchives.

Other places to search for records might be the VFW (Veterans of Foreign Wars) post where your veteran lived at the time of entering the war, as well as the local church or courthouse. Don't forget to look in the attic! You should also ask relatives, particularly elderly ones, who may have saved letters or mementos.

BIBLIOGRAPHY

Abzug, Robert H. *Inside the Vicious Heart: Americans and the Liberation of Nazi Concentration Camps.* New York: Oxford University Press, 1985.

Adkins, A. Z. Jr., and Andrew Z. Adkins III. *You Can't Get Much Closer Than This: Combat with Company H, 317th Infantry Regiment, 80th Division.* Havertown, PA: Casemate Publishing, 2005.

Allen, Robert S. *Lucky Forward: The History of General George Patton's Third U.S. Army.* New York: Vanguard Press, 1947.

Ambrose, Stephen E. *Citizen Soldiers: The U.S. Army from the Normandy Beaches to the Bulge to the Surrender of Germany, June 7, 1944, to May 7, 1945.* New York: Simon & Schuster, 1997.

———. *Band of Brothers: E Company, 506th Regiment, 101st Airborne from Normandy to Hitler's Eagle's Nest.* New York: Simon & Schuster, 1992.

Blumenson, Martin. *Breakout and Pursuit: United States Army in World War II.* Washington, D.C.: U.S. Army, Office of the Chief of Military History, 1961.

Brokaw, Tom. *The Greatest Generation.* New York: Random House, 1998.

Burhans, Robert D. *History and Heraldry of the 80th Division.* Richmond, VA: U.S. Army, 1960.

225

Carr, Walter P. "Perilous Patrol into Bastogne." *World War II* (1996): pp. 34–40.

Chamberlain, Brewster, and Marcia Feldman, eds. *The Liberation of the Nazi Concentration Camps, 1945: Eyewitness Accounts of the Liberators*. Washington, D.C.: United States Holocaust Memorial Council, 1987.

Cole, Hugh M. *The Ardennes: The Battle of the Bulge*. Washington, D.C.: U.S. Army, Office of the Chief of Military History, 1965.

———. *The Lorraine Campaign: United States Army in World War II*. Washington, D.C.: U.S. Army, Office of the Chief of Military History, 1965.

Contemporary History of Austria (1918–1955). Permanent exhibition of the Museum of Contemporary History in Ebensee, Austria, 2003.

Diagnostic and Statistical Manual of Mental Disorders, Fourth Edition, Text Revision. Washington, D.C.: American Psychiatric Association, 2000.

Doubler, Michael D. *Closing with the Enemy: How GIs Fought the War in Europe, 1944–1945*. Lawrence, Kans.: University Press of Kansas, 1994.

80th Infantry "Blue Ridge Division." Paducah, Ky.: Turner Publishing, second edition, 1991.

Fleming, Anne Taylor, interview on *Online NewsHour*, PBS, June 14 2001.

Fussell, Paul. *Doing Battle: The Making of a Skeptic*. Boston: Little, Brown, 1996.

———. *The Boys' Crusade: The American Infantry in Northwestern Europe, 1944–1945*. New York: Random House, 2003.

———. *Wartime: Understanding and Behavior in the Second World War*. New York: Oxford University Press, 1989.

Garcia, Max R. *As Long As I Remain Alive: The Autobiography of a Low-Number Survivor of Auschwitz.* Tuscaloosa, Ala.: Portals Press, 1979.

Gawne, Jonathan. *Finding Your Father's War: A Practical Guide to Researching and Understanding Service in the World War II US Army.* Drexel Hill, Penn.: Casemate Publishing, 2006.

Handy, Edward A., and Kemp Battle. *The Flame Keepers: The True Story of an American Soldier's Survival Inside Stalag 17.* New York: Ryperion, 2004.

Hastings, Max. *Armageddon: The Battle for Germany 1944–1945.* New York: Alfred A. Knopf, 2004.

Henshaw, Chester L. *A Record of Events: Company E, Second Battalion, 318th Infantry, 80th Infantry Division, World War II.* Palm Bay, Fla.: privately printed, 1993.

History—80th Infantry Division 1917–1944. Washington, DC: War Department, Adjutant General's Office, Unit History Reporting, March 10, 1945.

Janes, Terry D., producer. *Patton's Troubleshooters* (DVD and CD-ROM). Kansas City, Mis.: Opinicus Publishing, 2005.

Magee, Patricia Delnore, ed. *Victor's War: The World War II Letters of Lt. Col. Victor Delnore.* Paducah, Ky.: Turner Publishing Company, 2001.

Mauldin, Bill. *Up Front.* New York: Henry Holt and Company, 1945.

McManus, John C. *The Deadly Brotherhood: The American Combat Soldier in World War II.* Novato, Calif.: Presidio Press, 2000.

Murrell, Robert T., compiler. *317th Infantry Regiment History.* Oakridge, Penn.: privately printed, n.d.

———, compiler. *Stories of the Men of the 80th Division World War II Company M, 318th Regiment.* Oakridge, Penn.: privately printed, 2001.

————. *Operational History of the 80th Infantry Division, August 1944 to May 1945*. Oakridge, Penn.: privately printed, n.d.

————. *The Blue Ridge Division Answers the Call in WWII*. Oakridge, Penn.: privately printed, n.d.

Nichols, David, ed. *Ernie's War: The Best of Ernie Pyle's World War II Dispatches*. New York: Touchstone/Simon & Schuster, 1986.

O'Brien, Tim. "How War Changes the Warrior: Interview with Alex Chadwick," *Talk of the Nation*, PBS, November 11, 2004.

Patton, George S. *War as I Knew It*. Boston: Houghton Mifflin, 1947.

Pearson, Ralph E. *Enroute to the Redoubt: A Soldier's Report as a Regiment Goes to War, Vols. I-V*. Chicago: Adams Printing Service, 1958.

Pike, Thomas F., ed. *80th Infantry Division, September 1944, Moselle River Crossing, Parts I and II*. Washington, D.C.: Pike Military Research, n.d.

————. *80th Infantry Division, The Lorraine Campaign, November–Early December 1944*. Washington, D.C.: Pike Military Research, n.d.

Pyle, Ernie. *Brave Men*. New York: Henry Holt, 1944.

————. *Here Is Your War*. New York: Henry Holt, 1943.

Relinger, Eric. "Letter to Ulrich Koch of Athene TV, Berlin." Reprinted in *Blue Ridge Magazine* 84, No. 337 (Summer 2003).

Rosenheck, Robert, and Alan Fontana. "Transgenerational Effects of Abusive Violence on the Children of Vietnam Combat Veterans." *Journal of Traumatic Stress* 11, No. 4 (1998): 731–742.

Schnurr, P. P. "PTSD and Combat-Related Psychiatric Symptoms in Older Veterans." *PTSD Research Quarterly* 2, No. 1 (1991): pp. 1–6.

Turow, Scott, interview by Charlie Rose, *Charlie Rose*, PBS, November 8, 2005.

Van Ells, Mark D. *To Hear Only Thunder Again: America's World War II Veterans Come Home*. Lanham, Md.: Lexington Books, 2001.

Weigley, Russell F. *Eisenhower's Lieutenants: The Campaign of France and Germany, 1944–1945*. Bloomington: Indiana University Press, 1981.

Wilhelm, John. "Yanks Fight Bloody Battle to Cross Moselle in Rain: Infantrymen Open Hole for Patton's Tanks to Go Through," *Stars and Stripes* 4, No. 265 (September 8, 1944).

Websites

Combat Chronicle, 80th Infantry Division, U. S. Army Center for Military History: http://www.history.army.mil/lineage/cc/080id.htm

80th Infantry Division website (for division history, *After Action Reports, Morning Reports,* etc.): www.80thdivision.com

Ernie Pyle and his dispatches: www.journalism.indiana.edu/news/erniepyle

Forward 80th: The Story of the 80th Infantry Division, online version: www.lonesentry.com/gi_stories_booklets/80thinfantry/index.html

Patton's Troubleshooters, Terry D. Janes's website: www.thetroubleshooters.com

U.S. Army Center for Military History: www.army.mil

The author conducted interviews with the following World War II veterans and concentration camp survivors:

- George Anderson
- Walter Carr
- Aaron Cohen

- Jeannie Davis
- Robert Fasnacht
- Max Garcia
- Lloyd Jonnes
- Bill Kelly, Jr.
- Paul Mercer
- Robert Murrell
- Robert Persinger
- Leroy Pierce
- Patrick Stewart
- Clayton Warman

The full names of soldiers mentioned in my father's war journal are:

Lt. Theodore Ellsworth

Lt. Norval Graham

Lt. Walter Carr

Capt. Paul Chmar

Sgt. James Conroy

Col. John Golden

Sgt. Charles Roberts

Capt. Robert Matlick

Lt. Eugene Blanchard

Lt. Willie White

Lt. Santner (first name unknown)

Lt. Frank Congiolosi

Lt. Pete Rigg

INDEX